Dancing to the
Music in My Head

Dancing to the Music in My Head

Memoirs of the People's Idol

Sanjaya Malakar

with Alan Goldsher

POCKET BOOKS

New York London Toronto Sydney

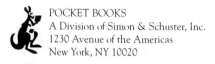
POCKET BOOKS
A Division of Simon & Schuster, Inc.
1230 Avenue of the Americas
New York, NY 10020

First Pocket Books hardcover edition February 2009

POCKET and colophon are registered trademarks of
Simon & Schuster, Inc.

For information about special discounts for bulk purchases,
please contact Simon & Schuster Special Sales at
1-800-456-6798 or business@simonandschuster.com.

Designed by Carla Little

Manufactured in the United States of America

10 9 8 7 6 5 4 3 2 1

Library of Congress Cataloging-in-Publication Data is available

ISBN-13: 978-1-4516-4161-5
ISBN-10:   1-4516-4161-3

First of all I want to thank the supreme spiritual personality that flows through every living thing. Some call it Jesus, or Krishna, or Buddha, or Allah, but it's all God. I would also like to thank my fans. Without their love and support I would not have the drive or energy to be able to pursue my dream. They deserve more credit and honor than I could ever give them, and for that I am thankful.

With Love,
Sanjaya

Acknowledgments

I would like to thank all of the people in my life who have helped me grow and evolve into the person I am today. First of all I have to thank my mother, Jillian Recchi, and my father, Vasudeva Malakar, for their continuous love and support throughout everything. To my sister, Shyamali, for always being there to help me and teach me through her experience and knowledge of the world. My stepmother Santana and my little brother Sri Nath for always being there for me and supporting everything I do. And my entire family for standing behind me in all my aspirations and keeping me grounded and levelheaded. Of course I have to thank everyone at *American Idol*. To Nigel Lythgoe and Ken Warwick for their guidance and support throughout my time on the show. I hope you know you made a wise decision. To the vocal coaches Debra Bird and Dorian Holly for keeping me on my toes and in the game even when I felt alone. To the pianists Michael Orland and Matt Rhode for giving me advice about singing, performing, and life. You made my goals seem possible. To everyone associated with the incredible machine that is *American Idol*, 19 Management, Fremantle Media, and all of you who supported us during the show and on tour, especially all the behind the scene workers. Thank you to all the agents at CAA. To Paula Abdul for always projecting positive, loving energy. To Randy Jackson for engaging with me and always making me feel comfortable. And of course, to Simon Cowell who, contrary to popular belief, I have great respect for and appreciate, for not being afraid to stand up and speak what's on his mind. I learned so much from all three of these people. They taught me to expand my horizons to places that we can only dream of and through that I have grown as a person and a professional. To my fellow contestants and friends, Jordin Sparks, Phil Stacey, LaKisha Jones, Gina Glocksen, and all the others I have met along the way. You taught me to dream and never give up. As my journey continues I keep meeting people who have so much knowledge and experience that I can learn and grow from. I'd like to thank my manager Frank Yandolino, who continues to create opportunities to expand my future horizons. To Barry Gruber for being there over the years. To my producer Gary Hasse for bringing in his funk and creativity to the music and helping me realize my full potential. Thank you Objective Entertainment and Jarred Weisfeld. And of course Alan Goldsher for his patience and understanding in the writing of this book. Thank you to everyone at Simon and Schuster, Louise Burke, Anthony Ziccardi, Megan McKeever,

Jean Anne Rose, and Lauren McKenna. I may have left people out, but to anyone I haven't mentioned, and to all the people I meet on the street every day, thank you for your love and support, and I hope that you receive all the good karma you deserve.

~PEACE~

Introduction

Something Good

My *American Idol* experience was a constant race against the clock. If I wanted to eat, I had to shove it down and then run right over to the next rehearsal, interview, meeting, shoot, or sound check. It was all *Get up at 7:00 a.m. and hurry to the van . . . then wait at the lot for forty minutes . . . then shoot some B-roll . . . then hurry back to the van . . . then wait at the studio . . . then hurry to the van . . . then wait for the mentor to show up.*

Since the producers and directors had to set up shots and locales—and because they wanted us to be available the second they were ready—we did a whole bunch of sitting around, chilling, talking, napping, and staring into outer space. We were sleep deprived, undernourished (or badly nourished, depending on your attitude toward catering), and stressed about auditioning for Simon Cowell, Paula Abdul, and Randy Jackson—aka the Big Three—show after show after show.

I think that part of the reason they ran us so ragged was to emotionally strip us. They wanted to see what we could do when we were at our most vulnerable. If our nerves were right at the surface, that could lead to onstage meltdowns, or off-stage drama, either of which would lead to better ratings. Also, they wanted to see how we could handle the pressure of having twenty-five hour-long commitments in a twenty-four-hour day. None of us knew if a successful (or even semisuc-cessful) career in the music industry would be that difficult, but at least we'd be prepared.

Nothing, however, could have prepared me for the How-ard Stern situation.

Howard Stern had gotten behind me, starting what he called the Sanjaya Revolution. He and his sidekick, Artie Lange, began a campaign to have the fans vote for me to stay on *Idol* again, and again, and again. I'm well aware he wasn't doing it because he loved my singing; it was because it made for good radio.

I never got a chance to listen to Howard Stern during *Idol*, but I wasn't completely blind to what the public and the media thought of me. The question has been asked, "Was Howard Stern the reason for my staying power on *American Idol*"? Howard was an unlikely campaigner who had been advising his fans to vote (in jest) for the first contestant of Indian descent to make it into the show's Top 12. From what

I understood, he'd called me his favorite contestant, and confessed he wanted to see me win.

Although I'd tried to avoid going online and seeing what the bloggers and the media were saying about me, I couldn't help but hear whispers about the general opinion of my singing. I realized that I wasn't as good (or as experienced) as the likes of such fellow contestants as Jordin Sparks, Phil Stacey, and Melinda Doolittle, but I thought that'd I'd been improving as a showman, and according to the Big Three, that's much of what *American Idol* is about: putting on a great show.

Phil Stacey

We never talked about what the bloggers or the media were writing about us, because we had bigger controversies at the time, specifically when our fellow contestant Antonella Barba's ex-boyfriend posted all those naked pictures of her on the Internet. We were too busy being mad at him to be concerned about the other stuff. We also talked a lot about another contestant, Sundance Head, because every rehearsal, he would blow us all away with his amazing voice, and then the cameras would turn on and something happened. It happened to all of us at one point or another, but, well, let's just say that Sundance was one of the best singers of the season.

All of which meant that this week—which was British Invasion Week—was even more important than the previous week . . . which had been even more important than the week before that . . . which was more crucial than the week before that. The pressure was building, and I knew that if I didn't come up with the best performance of the season—no, the best performance of my *life*—it was back to Seattle.

Really, I wasn't so concerned about going home—I had great friends and my sister, Shyamali, waiting for me, which would be wonderful. I just didn't want to blow my opportunity to hit the road. You see, the Top 10 finalists go on the two-month *American Idol* tour, a tour that would give me the opportunity to travel across the country and perform for thousands of people each night. Even though I was only seventeen and I had (fingers crossed) a long singing career ahead of me, there was absolutely no guarantee that I'd ever get a chance like that again, so I had to step my game up and make sure that Simon didn't trash me too badly, which might convince the viewers to let me go.

If I got cut, I'd move on to the next phase of my life, and that would be okay.

But you know what? I didn't want to get cut.

British Invasion Week, the brainchild of *Idol's* England-born executive producers Ken Warwick and Nigel Lythgoe, was the first week that I waited until the very very very very last minute to pick my song. Twenty-four hours before the performance, I hadn't decided whether to go with the Kinks' "You Really Got Me" or Herman's Hermits' "I'm into Something Good."

"I'm into Something Good" is a cheerful, poppy, feel-good kind of sappy tune that's supposed to make you happy all over. Lyrically speaking, "You Really Got Me" is equally feel-goody ("I always wanna be by your side / Girl, you really got me now / You got me so I can't sleep at night"—if you didn't know the melody, you might think it's a Bryan Adams bal-lad), but musically, it's more *grrrrrrrrr*. Crunchy guitars, hard-hitting drums, growly vocals; if I could pull it off without looking silly—and avoid people thinking *Oh, look at Sanjaya, Mr. All About Love, trying to get all gritty*—I might be in pretty good shape.

So I went with the rock song. Unfortunately, that week's mentor was none other than legendary Brit rocker Peter Noone, leader of Herman's Hermits. In my one-on-one meet-ing with Peter the day before the live telecast, after I told him I couldn't decide whether to sing his tune or the Kinks song, he said, "Well, I'm a bit biased. If you did Herman's Hermits, that would certainly make me look good. But you choose what you'd like."

After I finished performing both tunes for Peter, and after he told me that I'd done a good job, he seemed kind of disap-pointed when I explained that I'd decided to go with the Kinks. I felt a little badly about rejecting his song right in front of his face, but I felt in my gut that "You Really Got Me" would give me a better chance to survive. Peter was cool about it, though, and gave me some good advice: "If you're going to sing the Kinks, you really have to go for it. You have to go all the way there. Don't be afraid." Paula had said the same thing several times over the past eight weeks, but it made a bigger impact on me to hear it come from a guy who was friends with Ray and Dave Davies.

My song selection surprised most everybody associated with the show. They probably didn't think I could do justice to a Kinks song, because I was the mellow crooner guy who, when it came to choreography, walked around the stage and did a little Gospel Rock dance move. To them, "Sanjaya" and "garage rock 'n' roll" didn't add up.

During dress rehearsal, I ran through "You Really Got Me," and it felt all wrong. Maybe everybody was right. Maybe I wasn't that guy. Maybe I wasn't a rock singer. Maybe it wasn't my thing.

But I took Peter Noone's suggestions and went for it, went all the way there. As a matter of fact, I went *farther* than all the way there, jumping off the stage, running through the aisles, generally acting the rock 'n' roll fool. The arrangement ended on three percussive hits—*Bap! Bap! Bap!*—during which I leapt back onstage and fell right on my butt, then raised my arms to the sky, as if falling on my butt was my plan from the get-go.

Ken and Nigel stared at me, frozen. It looked to me from the stage like they were freaking out, but I wasn't sure if it was out of happiness or horror. I was certain, though, that they never expected that sort of energy burst out of me. How could they have known that when we Malakars get excited, we get *excited*. It's a heredity deal.

After a few moments of awkward silence, Ken cleared his throat and said, "Um, wow. Wow. Wow. I didn't even know you could do that. And, um, I don't even know if you should try that. Maybe you should go with Herman's Hermits."

The last thing I wanted to do at that point was kick into "Woke up this mornin' feelin' fine / There's somethin' special on my mind"—after having fun with the grungy Kinks song, it would be hard to be all cheerful with the Hermits—but I was a good soldier, so I gave it a shot. But I wasn't *that* good of a soldier; I completely overdid the song and cheesed it up as if it was a piece from a Broadway show. In other words, I tanked it.

Ken rolled his eyes and said, "Do whatever song you want."

I'm sure he had plenty of other fires to put out and didn't have the time to argue with me about tune selection. He probably thought that if I got voted off, it was my own fault.

Since I was planning an all-out performance, I wanted to keep my style relatively simple, but still be bold. The stylist found a gray jacket with the alphabet printed all over it, and we built around that. We kept the hair natural so I could toss it while I ran around. I thought it looked good.

And apparently, so did the Crying Girl.

Ashley Ferl, aka the Crying Girl, was a pale-skinned, blond-haired, blue-eyed preteen from Riverside, California. She and her parents won tickets to the March 21, 2007, *Idol* dress rehearsal, and they got themselves some great seats; they were close enough to the stage that I could read her hand-drawn sign: MY DREAM IS TO MEET SANJAYA.

As the contestants and I lined up onstage for our weekly introductions, I gave Ashley a little wave, and she immediately started crying. The producers noticed, and thought having her bawl during my performance would make for a great *Idol* moment, so they gave her tickets to the live show and hoped for the best. I decided to use this to my advantage. She would be a responsive soul to sing to, and I thought that her energy would help my energy.

Jordin Sparks

I don't think she stopped bawling for six hours. He said to me, "I have no idea what to do about this." I said, "She's your fan, Sanjaya. You should be psyched."

Even though the Kinks tune was set in stone, there was still some confusion among the team, so when *Idol* host Ryan Seacrest introduced me that night, he said, "Well, singing either 'You Really Got Me' or 'I'm into Something Good,' here's Sanjaya Malakar." I prayed to have the energy to make it through the song, and then bolted onto the stage.

On a certain level, I didn't even care what the judges thought. This week I was doing it for myself. I was going to be free. If I was going to get cut, I wanted to at least be able to say that I put my heart into it. Anything that happened beyond that was out of my control.

From note one, I incorporated Peter Noone's suggestions and tried to channel the Kinks. I purposely oversang and sneered my way through the first verse, so I sounded as if I'd been drinking and smoking and not sleeping for weeks. (The fact that practically everybody on the show had a killer cold and a runny nose all week, myself included, made it that much easier to come across as throaty.) Since my hair was nice and loose, I flopped it around, not quite to the point of headbanging, but enough so that there was some noticeable movement. The audience was on their feet and clapping, far more enthusiastic about me than they'd been the entire season.

And the good news for the producers was that Ashley got more into it than they could've hoped for. She cried and cried and cried, and was having trouble catching her breath, so much trouble, in fact, that she wasn't able to clap in rhythm on two and four. And the cameras captured it for all eternity.

I ran around the stage almost as much as I did during dress rehearsal, and it affected my vocals, particularly my intonation, but I didn't care. That night was about performance. During the second verse, I took a chance: I walked onto the table behind the judges. I wasn't sure that that was the right move until Paula, who was bopping around in her chair, waggled her fingers right in front of my face. That jazzed me up. At least I had one of them on my side.

And then it was time to sing for Ashley. But being that the arrangement was only two minutes long, I had to do a quick walk-by. When I saw the tape later, I realized the producers were right: crying girls make for good television.

On the final verse, the entire band except for the drummer dropped out, so it was just me and the groove. I whispered the lines, hoping I sounded evil and mysterious. Then when the rest of the rhythm section came back in, I screamed the lyrics. I'm not sure if people liked it, but it sure felt good. And then I did my little jumps on the outro and, thankfully, managed to not land on my butt.

The crowd's response was more muted than it had been in the past, probably because they didn't know what hit them. *What was that about? Who was that kid yelling all over the place? Was that really our little, sweet, gentle Sanjaya?* My guess was that they were totally confused. The Big Three, on the other hand, were another story. Randy gave a *whoop*. Paula gave a *whoo*. Simon cracked a teeny-tiny smile. It was the best reception I'd ever had from them.

Randy, as usual, started things off. "Yo, man, listen, all right? I've got to tell you, you shocked me tonight." I thought, *Uh-oh. Does "shock me" mean he hated it more than anything I've done before?* He continued, "Usually, you're this kind of reserved, just kind of this mildly meek kind of cool guy. And you came out of your shell tonight. That was your best performance to date, baby." He turned to his left and said, "I'm in shock, Paula."

See? I made it all about performance, and it worked.

Paula said, "That's what we've been waiting for."

Randy said, in a silly, booming voice, "It's the new San-jaya."

Paula said, "*Yeeeeeeeeahhhh!* Go for it. Go for it. You went for it. It was a lot of fun. I like this. I hope you had fun up there."

"I did." I'd been having fun onstage for the last two months, but I guess they hadn't felt my vibe from the table.

Paula gave me one of her cute little rounds of applause, then Randy, still shocked, I suppose, cracked up and said, "Oh-oh-oh-oh God." I'm not sure I wanted to know what that was about.

Then Simon, who, shocker of shockers, was smiling, gestured over to Ashley and said, "I think the little girl's face says it all." And that was it. Unbelievable. I'd rendered Simon Cowell speechless . . . and in a good way. I put my heart into the song, and I think he recognized that. Yay!

And then over came Ryan. He gestured over to Ashley and said to Simon, "I actually think she liked him."

Simon said, "Really?"

"Yeah," Ryan said, then asked Ashley, "You liked that, right? It was good? You're a fan?" All Ashley could do was nod, smile, and raise her hands up in the air. Ryan said to me, "Why don't you go say hi to this little girl?" then turned back to Ashley. "What's your name?"

"Ashley."

"Ashley, great." He gently ushered me out into the audience. "Ashley, this is Sanjaya. Sanjaya, this is Ashley."

As I gave her a little hug, Randy, who had suddenly become my biggest fan, let out a long "A*wwwwwwwwwwwwwwwww!*"

After the hug, Ryan asked Ashley, "Are you having fun? Do you need anything?" Confused, she shook her head. "Well, if you do, let us know. We'll be right here." Ryan was all about trying to make people feel at ease, to relax them, to make them happy.

Unfortunately, he wasn't able to make my fellow contestant Stephanie Edwards happy. Stephanie, who'd sung what I thought was a stellar version of Dusty Springfield's "You Don't Have to Say You Love Me," was voted off by the viewers. As for me, despite having been Simon Cowell's punching bag for the last month, I lived to fight another week.

But truthfully, I wasn't sure how much fight I had left.

PART ONE

The Family or *Vaha Kutumba* or *La Famiglia*

I may not look it, but mentally, physically, and ethnically speaking, I'm just as much Italian as I am Indian: family oriented, opinionated, emotional, a lover of eggplant Parmesan, and honest to a fault . . . and sometimes quite loud.

That all comes from my mother's side of the family. My grandfather, Joseph Paul Recchi Sr., was born and raised in Seattle, a first-generation Italian-American whose parents came together on a boat from Italy. He worked for Seattle City Light, the main utility company for the city, for more than thirty years, rising up from an entry-level position to superintendent. He was nonjudgmental and benevolent, the kind of guy who would sincerely ask how you were doing, and sincerely listen to the answer. I'd like to think I'm the same way.

My mom, Jillian Recchi, was also born and raised in Seattle. She had three brothers and two sisters before her parents got divorced; then her mom had three more kids, a girl and two boys, which gives Mom a total of eight siblings, all of whom have always lived in or around Seattle. Okay, maybe not always: every once in a while, one of my family members would move to Hawaii, or Italy, or New York, or Montana, or Oregon, or North Dakota, or California, or Canada, or Belize . . . you know, the usual. Although there was often at least one family member missing from Seattle, we always came back. The Recchis recognize and respect the importance of keeping the family unit together.

My dad, Vasudeva Malakar, was born in Vrindavan, India, and was raised by his aunt and uncle until he was put in an ashram boarding school called Gurukula when he was five years old. There, he studied to become a Brahman, which is a Hindu holy man. He came to America as part of the International Society for Krishna Consciousness Hindu temple.

For a guy from India, Dad was pretty street savvy. When I was in fourth grade, I lived with him for a few months in Berkeley, California, but in the bad part of Berkeley, a few blocks away from the Oakland ghetto. The day we heard gunshots right outside, Dad knew exactly where and how to duck in order to avoid any stray bullets. It was the first time I'd spent any significant time in the 'hood, and I'm actually glad I had a chance to live there, because it made me realize how fleeting and precious life can be. That said, you shouldn't live your life every day like you're going to die tomorrow. You have to find a balance. That's not the kind of thing that too many fourth graders get an opportunity to learn.

Mom and Dad met the day he got off the plane from India at the ISKCON temple in San Francisco, just up the hill from Haight-Ashbury. She was eighteen and he was twenty-one. They clicked in part because they were both instrumentalists and singers. My mother plays jazz flute, clarinet, soprano sax, and violin (we still have her violin, and every once in a while, I'll pull the tiny thing out and imagine three-year-old Jill Recchi fumbling through her scales), and my father is a classical Indian singer and plays a number of classical Indian instruments, including the harmonium and the mridanga. Considering my artistic genes, it would've been more of a surprise to everybody had I *not* become a musician of some sort. They were married five years later. Two years after that, my sister Shyamali was born; then two years after that, I came around.

Despite having had two kids, Mom is still unbelievably youthful looking, which isn't surprising, because she's always been very careful about what she puts into her body. She eats only organic food and drinks only filtered water, and it's totally working for her. You want proof? Soon after the *Idol* tour, she came with me to a comedy club in New York, and I introduced her to a bunch of my friends, and quite a few of them gave her an intense up-and-down look, pulled me aside, and said, "Say what?!? That's your *mother*?!? She's a total hottie!" I'm not going to lie: that was awkward. I mean, I recognize my mom is beautiful—she's in her early forties but looks like she's in her midtwenties. She's very outgoing—she's Italian, remember—youthful, and approachable . . . but I still can't think of her as a hottie. She's my mom. (It's kind of the same thing with my sister. I recognize she's a beautiful young lady, but the words "Shyamali" and "hottie" kind of don't go together for me.)

Growing up, we lived in an apartment in the building that my great-grandfather bought after he came over from Italy. At one point or another, seemingly every member of my family lived in that place. Sometimes there'd be an aunt living in the unit above us, and a bunch of cousins below, and then a year later the cousins would be on the top floor, and there'd be an uncle on the ground level. It was a continuously rotating family house.

Shyamali and I regularly hung out with all thirteen of our first cousins (are you ready for the list? From oldest to youngest: Chandra, Ambyr, Camila, Makenzie, Alyssa, Giovanni, Giuseppe, Dominic, Isabella, Alex, Ahmanni, Kayla, and Deja), not because we were forced to but because we wanted to, because being with our family filled our souls with joy. Many of them are singers, songwriters, musicians, painters, or sculptors, and back in the day, Makenzie, Alyssa, and I would put on choreographed miniconcerts of Disney tunes. At holidays, the whole family sang and danced around my grandfather's baby grand piano, using the fireplace as a stage. Thanksgiving and Christmas get-togethers at Grandpa's house were like an Italian Lollapalooza.

Shyamali Malakar

Our parents weren't pushers of the arts. When I told Mom that I wanted to be in the theater, she helped me pursue it. But they never forced us into it; they know it's a stressful business and it's hard to succeed. She actually would've preferred if I'd have done something less unpredictable. But that's what Sanjaya and I gravitated toward. We couldn't help it.

My parents got divorced when I was three and Shyamali was five and a half. The divorce wasn't too ugly—it wasn't like they couldn't be in the same room together. They actually remained close friends, so close that Mom helped Dad's second wife get acclimated to the United States after she moved here from India, and she also let my father live in her house while he was saving money to get my younger brother and stepmom over from India. Those aren't the kinds of things that too many women would do for their ex-husbands.

Also, they had me and Shyamali in common, so when we ended up living with my mother, there wasn't ever any weirdness when Dad came to pick us up each weekend. Though we lived with Mom, my Indian side remained alive and well; Dad might not have been around that much, but his influence and the Indian culture were always there, most notably when it came to music and spirituality.

Shyamali and I have never really spoken in-depth about the divorce, but frankly, we didn't have to. We're unbelievably close, and we're kind of able to read each other's mind: sometimes words aren't necessary. The psychic thing also comes in handy when we're hanging out with friends or doing interviews, or when I'm in the middle of making a random point and I lose my train of thought. She'll jump in and finish my sentence, and it'll be totally accurate, almost exactly what I would've said . . . although maybe she'll say it a little more articulately. We've always depended on each other, and the divorce wasn't as bad as it could've been for us, because we had each other to lean on. She always has my back, and even though she's the older sister, I look out for her. Our relationship is so tight that sometimes when we're together, everybody else in the world is on the outside.

Shyamali is supersmart, and has been so since the beginning. My grandmother owned a store that sold crystals and incense and all kinds of cool little trinkets, and once in a while she'd stick Shyamali up at the front counter, put a dictionary in front of her, and say, "Okay sweetie, go." And then my three-year-old sister would read a word and its definition perfectly, and my grandmother would clap her hands and scream, "Yaaaay!" (My grandmother, by the way, was a free-spirited hippie back in the 1960s and 1970s. She was part of the "Save the Earth" movement. And she embraced healthy living and organic eating.)

As tight as Shyamali and I were, there were still moments when our sibling rivalry would rear its ugly head. Once when I was six, my sister and I were fighting about the kind of stupid stuff that six- and eight-year-olds fight about, and she said something that got me so angry, I whipped a deck of cards at her. I threw the deck so hard that the cards traveled all the way across the living room and hit her in the temple. She passed out for a few seconds, which was long enough for me to think I had killed her. Watching her fall broke my heart, and that's all I needed to see to learn my lesson.

Shyamali Malakar

We didn't get along that well until we got older. We spent most of our childhood fighting with each other. I was always too cool for school, and he was always annoying, because all little brothers are uncool and annoying. I'd go off with my friends all the time, and that was the catalyst for a lot of problems. Like the Super Soaker.

Okay, maybe I didn't *entirely* learn my lesson. One weekend about three years later, she had a few friends over, and I was jealous that she was paying attention to them rather than to me, so while they were in the room, I filled up my Super Soaker and emptied it under her door. They were flooded out of the room to the tune of one inch of water. Of course, that stunt got me grounded.

But I wasn't always the one who started making trouble. Sometimes when we argued, she outthought me and manipulated the conversation so that I would get furious and act out. I think that's a natural older sister–younger brother thing, which is why it's sometimes tough being baby bro.

Shyamali Malakar

I have a really big moth phobia. It's totally irrational. I'm not scared of the dark, and I'm not scared of spiders, but moths are weird, and they gross me out. For fun, Sanjaya used to catch three or four of them in his hand, then throw them into my face. He thought it was the greatest thing.

After my parents' divorce was finalized, we moved into an amazing house in Bothell, Washington, just north of Seattle. And then the summer between first and second grade we moved to the beautiful island of Kauai, Hawaii. Hawaii was wonderful except for the fact that we lived on a teeny-tiny island and everybody knew everything about everyone. As much as I love people, it's sometimes nice to have some secrets. Even in second grade, I didn't like when people I barely knew were all up in my business.

Another problem for me was that in Hawaii, Shyamali began to blossom. She became one of the most popular girls in school, and I lost my identity. I was no longer Sanjaya; I was Shyamali's brother. She was supermature and super-smart—she was so far ahead of other kids that she skipped second grade and seventh grade—and was hanging out with kids who were four, five, and six years older than she was . . . which meant she wasn't hanging out with me. I couldn't really blame her for blowing me off, though. If all my friends were older, wiser, and more grownup, I'd probably ignore my little sibling too.

Shyamali and I were both in an acting group called the Hawaii Children's Theatre, and Shyamali went overseas with them twice, first in 1998 to the World's Fair in Lisbon, Portugal, then to the 2000 World's Fair in Hanover, Germany. It most definitely wasn't your typical theater troupe. On their first European trip, they'd wander the streets as a unit, then every once in a while the director would stop them and yell, "*Okay, go!*" And then they'd launch into a series of skits about saving the whales, or they'd sing songs about how you shouldn't pollute, or they'd perform in the name of some other earth-friendly cause. In Germany, it was the same deal, except this time the plays were about teenage romance. They wrote several pieces about a group of superheroes called the Power Pore Girls, whose job it was to swoop in and save poor students from the horror of having to attend the prom with a zit on their chin. Apparently, acne was a problem in Europe, because the crowds ate it up.

Shyamali is a jack-of-all-artistic-trades, and she's inspired me to be the same. Music is the seed that has grown and engulfed the very core of my soul, but I was also encouraged in other areas of art: I enjoy ceramics, drawing, design, poetry, dance, and theater.

Shyamali Malakar

I started getting serious about musical theater when I was ten, and that's around when Sanjaya and I started vibing on a musical level. He wasn't old enough to be in the programs that I was in, but he came to my rehearsals every day, and he learned every dance move, and every word to every song, and every line of dialogue. And when an actor forgot a line, Sanjaya would yell it out to them. Even then, everybody knew he wanted to be an entertainer.

But songs are at the top of my artistic loves. I was listening to Stevie Wonder, Earth, Wind & Fire, and Bob Marley while I was in the womb. I always have music running through my brain, and sometimes, while I'm standing on a corner waiting for a stoplight to change, or I'm wandering into a grocery store, or waiting to be seated at a restaurant, I'll hear, for instance, "Like a fool I went and stayed too long / Now I'm wondering if your love's still strong," and I'll start moving in rhythm, sometimes just bobbing my head, sometimes all-out boogying. When somebody asks, "What're you doing?" I'll say, "I'm dancing to the music in my head." It was sometimes a problem in school, especially in the middle of a test, when I'd too loudly hum a snatch of "Is This Love," "Get Up, Stand Up," or "No Woman, No Cry." Some of my classmates loved it, some didn't appreciate it, but either way, I couldn't help it. There's always music in me, and if I couldn't get it out, I'd probably explode.

School Dazed

We moved around a lot, mostly within Seattle. The family building I was born in was on Capitol Hill, in downtown Seattle. From there we moved north of Seattle to Bothell, to a huge house on a two-acre plot of land, one acre of which was beautiful, lush wetlands. This property bordered Department of Natural Resources land, which gave us unlimited open land and woods to play in.

In Hawaii, we lived in a house we bought on an acre of property filled with every tropical fruit imaginable: mangos, papayas, passion fruit, jackfruit, noni, five varieties of bananas, oranges, avocados, and coconuts. When we went back to the mainland, we moved back into our home in Bothell, after which I lived with my aunt in Shoreline, Washington, and then we moved to our home in Federal Way, about thirty minutes south of Seattle. If nothing else, I learned how to pack up my stuff quickly and efficiently.

Aside from coffee and music, Seattle is known mostly for its rain and generally bad weather. Most residents don't appreciate a good storm, but I love it. For me, the rain, the clouds, and the wind are all beautiful. There's constant precipitation nine months out of the year, and it depresses a lot of people, but I think I had a pretty healthy attitude toward bad weather. Sometimes during a crashing thunderstorm, while everybody is running inside, huddling under an umbrella, or hiding under an awning, I'll fly outside to chill with the intense showers. And I wasn't ever particularly affected by the cold; I had no problem going downtown and playing in the snow, wearing nothing but shorts and a T-shirt. All the coffee-drinking Seattleites would stare at me and think, *What is up with this kid?* This isn't to say that I don't love Seattle's three dry, temperate months. Everything is green and warm and sweet-smelling. It's just like Southern California . . . except you can breathe the air. For those Seattleites who don't appreciate a good downpour, I'm sure the spring and summer beauty somewhat make up for those several dark, rainy fall and winter months.

I ended up being enrolled in ten different schools in ten years. Whenever I switched schools, it was usually for one of two main reasons: (1) my family had moved to a new school district, or (2) I wasn't challenged or working hard enough for anybody's good.

My lack of interest in studying had nothing to do with how smart I was or wasn't. I understood everything my teachers were saying, but it bored me out of my mind. The constant litany was, "Sanjaya, you get all these great test scores. Why don't you do your homework?"

I'd say something like, "I guess I'm sorry that I'm smart but I'm not trying. I want to learn about being a marine biologist, or a zoologist, or something. I don't care about grammar." (I'm sure that my English teachers will be shocked to see that I've managed to write an entire book.) Shyamali and I were both always interested in animals, and she knew the answer to any question you'd have about any animal. Ask her, "How big is a dolphin?" and she'll say, "They can be as small as four feet, and as big as thirty feet, and the word 'dolphin' is derived from the ancient Greek word for 'womb.' " And it wasn't like she spent a lot of time studying this kind of thing—she just kind of knew it.

After a long day of trying to stay focused in class, I'd go home and stare at my textbook, and if I came across something interesting to read, I'd read it, and if there was an interesting math or science problem, I'd solve it. But something usually distracted me, like a piece of music coming from my mother's stereo, or the sound of a particularly intense Seattle rainstorm. Sometimes a crack in the ceiling was more interesting than my social studies homework. I'm not saying this was the right way to go about grade school, but I couldn't help it. My brain went where my brain went, no matter how much I wanted to do the right thing. I can't even blame television or video games; we hardly ever had a TV around the house, so I couldn't watch, say, *American Idol* . . . or any other show, for that matter. And no television also meant no Nintendo. I wasn't totally deprived; I had a Game Boy, and sometimes I would fall into a Tetris trance, but that was it. (Once in a while I'd crave some Mario action, and fortunately a good percentage of my eighteen cousins had a gaming system, so a game fix was only a short car ride away.)

There were a few things I liked about school. I enjoyed doing multimedia projects, and as a Virgo, I always tried to make everything perfect, which often worked against me. In seventh grade, at an alternative public school called Northshore Junior High, I was in honors science, and we were assigned to put together a presentation on purifying water. Our task was to figure out how to take nasty sewage water and decontaminate it so it was safe to return to the regular water supply. I did a big old research essay and printed it out on fancy paper, and I did up a display demonstrating how to make the water nice and clean. But I went into Virgo mode—checking, double-checking, and triple-checking every little thing—and ended up turning it in two days late. The science teacher skimmed the paper and glanced at my display. Then he nodded, smiled, and said, "Sanjaya, this is wonderful. You get a hundred percent." Then he paused, and said, "Or at least you would've gotten a hundred if you'd have turned it in on time. As it is, I have to give you a fifty."

In spite of my dislike of homework, I tested well enough to get into mostly honors-level classes, which were a bit more challenging, but it was basically just the same curriculum that had bored me for five years, except with more homework, which—because of my homework issues—defeated the purpose for me. I was a great test-taker, though, which frustrated my teachers, because they thought I had potential. I drove them a bit nuts.

Most of the teachers didn't get me—or appreciate that I'd be sitting in the back of their classroom, drawing a picture in my sketchbook, more or less ignoring what they were saying but correctly answering every question I was asked—but some of them were really cool and understood that I was more artistic than academic. They'd invite me to their office at lunch and go over what I wasn't getting, and they were patient, and they *understood*. They recognized I had a brain, but they also saw that it was taking me in another direction. If more one-on-one attention were given to disinterested grade school students, junior high would be a way happier place for everybody.

One of my teachers recommended that my mother and I go visit the school counselor, because the teacher was curious why I tested off the charts but could not focus either in class or on my homework. We went two weeks later, and after an hour of chatting, the counselor peered at my file, then at me, then at my mother, and said, "I'd like to evaluate your son to see if he has ADHD. He may be struggling with this condition and we think that you should probably put him on Ritalin." (They called it ADHD. I called it having an artistic soul.)

Mom didn't agree with a word of what the counselor said, probably because when she was in school, she was also bored out of her mind with what her teachers were throwing at her, so she could relate to what I was feeling and going through. She told the counselor, "Nope. I'm not going to put my kid on drugs. There're plenty of other things we can do to make him more focused." I agreed.

You see, it's not impossible to make me focus. Give me a pair of headphones and a little more time and I'll have your assignment done, no problem. That said, I could see why the counselor thought I had the disorder. I've always been energetic, and I'm easily distracted, but that kind of label would tell the world that I have what some consider to be a disease, and would define me to other people. It wasn't fair to turn me from Sanjaya the Chill Arty Kid to Sanjaya the Hyperactive Blow-off.

It wasn't about a disorder. It was about my diverse interests—there are sooooo many things I'm interested in outside of what they teach you at school that when I come across something that doesn't fit into that plan, I drift, distracted by the need to quench that passion for art in general: drama, drawing, music, ceramics, dance, poetry. I could go on all day.

When you think about it, everybody has a bit of ADHD or ADD in them.

The New Kid in School . . . Again

I've always loved meeting new people, so moving from school to school was easier for me than it probably was for a lot of people. But some moves were harder than others, because I was the only brown kid there. When I introduced myself around some of the whiter schools, my new classmates would stare at my dark skin and say, "Hi, San . . . San . . . *SanWhatUh?*"

But for the most part, the transitions were pretty smooth, if a little bit awkward. In eighth grade, I went to a private school called Seattle Waldorf where all sixteen students had been in the same class, with the same teacher, since kindergarten. They'd been together forever, and I was late to the party . . . *very* late. Day one, I was like, "Hiiiii, I'm Sanjaya," and they were like, "Whatever." But at least they pronounced it correctly.

I figured I'd feel like an outcast for the entire year, but my second day there, we dived into a class project in which we boxed up a bunch of clothing to send to needy countries. It was an unbelievably nice thing to do—we never did any noteworthy charity work at any of the public schools I'd been to—but to be honest, it was a bit tedious. On the plus side, it gave me an opportunity to get to know some of my new classmates, and we got really tight really fast, so tight that they'd sometimes forget I was the new guy.

Soon the other kids were asking me questions like, "Remember in the fourth grade when we went to blah-blah-blah?" I'd have to remind them, "I've only been here for three months." But it was awesome to get so close with these people so quickly. They already had solid relationships, but they were cool enough to pull me right on in.

The girls also made me one of their own. I was raised with women, and I'd developed the ability to communicate with and understand girls as well as, if not better than, boys. I'd learned the code. (Sometimes I still get it wrong, but I think I'm better than average.)

Since I could both talk and listen to the girls, they tended to come to me with their problems. (A lot of the guys speculated that since I hung out with the girls, and wasn't into sports, I was gay. I told them, "Um, okay, believe what you want." They were the ones who were missing out. They had the jock straps. I had the girls.) I helped them as best I could, but sometimes I wondered, *Why me? I want to make you happy, but I have problems too. I don't necessarily want to spend all of my energy saving the female population of the school.* But I was too nice to turn anybody away, so I became an unpaid, unacknowledged counselor for a bunch of thirteen-year-old emo chicks.

These kids had spent their early school years focusing on the arts, which was cool because, well, it's the arts, and art of any sort is intrinsically cool. However, that was tough for the kids who were slower academically, because when they fell behind, it took them a year or two to catch up.

For their first two years at Waldorf, life for these kids was all about making stuff—if you wanted a toy to play with, you couldn't bring in something your parents had bought at a store; you had to create it yourself—and they didn't start teaching reading until second grade. My cousin Camilla went through the program and came out beautifully, but her brother Giuseppe didn't pick up things as quickly. His Waldorf teachers wouldn't admit that their program wasn't perfect for all of their students, so their attitude was "Oh, he's a little bit of a troubled child. He's ADD. He's easily distracted. He longs for attention. He's the devil child. We can't deal with him." So they kicked him out.

I knew exactly how he felt.

School Dazed, Part II

Even though I had reservations about it, I tested to get into a high school in Seattle called the Northwest School of the Arts. The test was meant to find out where I was at academically, as well as the level and quality of my artistic mindset. There were three sections: multiple choice (standard academic questions that you would find on any assessment test), short answer (more of the same, but a bit more arts based), and an essay about politics. I felt great about the way I handled the first two parts, but when I got to the essay page, I chewed on my pencil and thought, *I don't really want to go to this school. It would be really cool to go to a private arts school, but I kind of want to have my little public school experience.*

So I botched the essay. It wasn't too hard to botch, honestly; if my mother didn't have Air America Radio playing around the house all the time, I probably wouldn't have known *anything* about politics. After I blew the exam, I ended up moving in with my cousin in the northern part of Seattle, and I went to Shorecrest High School.

Shorecrest didn't have the greatest reputation. Like if you told one of the private school kids about it, they'd say, "*What?!* You're going to *Shorecrest?!?* Yikes." It was an average school filled with what I liked to call suburban gangsters. It was ghetto, even though we weren't in the ghetto.

I eased my way into the Shorecrest routine. I'd gotten into the habit of sitting in the back of the class and being really quiet when I started at a new school; maybe I'd chime in with an answer, but mostly I'd be low-key. Within two to three weeks, I'd start to let my true personality come through: loud, fun-loving, and, well, sometimes kind of obnoxious. I'd make jokes with my classmates and get into long debates with the teachers.

My freshman geography class featured one of the more lively debates of my Shorecrest career. My teacher moved all the desks out of the way and put five lines on the floor with masking tape. He explained that he would offer up a situation or rule and we would each go to one of the tape lines, depending on whether we strongly agreed, agreed, disagreed, strongly disagreed, or were neutral.

Things were going along perfectly smoothly until the teacher asked, "Do you believe that students should be obligated to respect their teacher no matter what?" Most of the class went to the agree and strongly agree lines. It's kind of a touchy subject when you're being asked by your teacher if you should respect him, so some people played it safe. Not me. I went into battle mode, strutting over to the strongly disagree area.

I know this may sound like I was being obstinate, but hear me out:

The teacher asked me to explain myself, because I was the only one who strongly disagreed. I said that the reason I was on that line was because I didn't like the wording of the question. I don't think anyone should be *obligated* to respect anyone no matter what. There's a certain amount of respect that a superior of any kind deserves because of his or her position and experience, but in general, respect has to be earned.

I spent a good fifteen or twenty minutes breaking down this point to the smallest detail, and by the end, the class had divided evenly among the lines. Success.

Sometimes my teachers were chill about my behavior, but most of the time they weren't, and it affected my grades. I got passable grades in ceramics, science, and choir, but by the end of freshman year, I had become so overwhelmed trying to pass the other classes that I slacked on the easier courses, and my grade point average was so low that they wanted me to repeat the ninth grade.

That wasn't going to happen. One trip through ninth grade was enough.

I enrolled in and paid for seven online classes—biology 1 and 2, English, math, Spanish, French, and geography—and was eventually able to test into sophomore classes, although I was still technically a freshman.

Sophomore year I went to a school in Federal Way, about thirty minutes south of Seattle, called Todd Beamer High School. At this school, we had to be in our seats at seven twenty, which was hell. My bus came at six thirty. Since I had to walk to my stop, this meant a five thirty wake-up call. On the way to the bus, I'd look at the sky and think, *Ohmigod, where's the sun? The sun isn't out, and I'm awake. This isn't right.* It was miserable. (I never was a morning person. When I was a baby, I would stay up all day and not nap, then at night I couldn't fall asleep. Even as an infant, I was a night owl with a rock-star internal body clock.)

I wasn't one of the really popular guys, but I acted like I was the most popular kid in the city. I'd walk down the hall with the group who yelled, screamed, and laughed, and I'd be the one right up front, one of the ringleaders. I was a floater; I hung with everybody from the Goths, the emos, the alterna-kids, the punks, and the stoners, to the jocks, the brains, the drama geeks, the mathletes, and the loners. Our school lunch-room had two floors, and the jocks, the cheerleaders, and the preps—the stereotypical "good kids"—ate upstairs, and the "bad kids" chilled out downstairs. We actually called ourselves the Downstairs Kids.

The downstairs crew always welcomed me with open arms even though I was the new kid, mostly because we were simi-lar. We were alternative, creative, open-minded people who didn't want to be stuck in a box. We were free. But that didn't stop me from going upstairs once in a while. I dig people, and I'll hang with anybody if they're chill.

As a floater, I always felt bad for the kids who didn't have too many friends, and I made it a point to try to bring them into my circles. Sometimes it worked, and sometimes it didn't, but I always did my best to include them. I often found myself having to move from group to group because I was neutral and some of the other kids weren't. I got some heat for it, but I didn't care. I was enjoying life and making as many friends as I could.

And that's all that mattered . . . that is, except for music.

Soul Power

My musical growth is ongoing and ever changing, largely because I've been exposed to an eclectic mix of styles and influences. (Thanks, Mom and Dad.) I've always craved obscure and unknown sounds and artists so I could feel where different vibes were coming from.

There's so much I never would've understood about life if I'd never heard certain songs—for instance, Amos Lee's "Arms of a Woman." It's a really simple, really beautiful folk ballad—it isn't a typical verse-chorus-verse format, but rather mostly chorus, which is part of the reason why it sticks in your head even if you've heard it only once—that I first heard performed by an *Idol* contestant named Tommy Daniels. Listening to Tommy croon "I am at ease in the arms of a woman /

Although now, most of my days, I spend alone," I thought, *Wow, this guy has soul. And this song has soul.* And thanks to my family's artistic DNA, I've fortunately always been able to recognize and appreciate true soulfulness.

Even somebody who doesn't have soul realizes that soul isn't always present in the world of *American Idol.* A lot of performers who audition for *Idol* tend to forget the emotion of a song and focus on technique. They oversing because they feel that that's the only way they'll be able to make a good impression on the judges and the voters in the short amount of time they're allotted. They want to show off everything they can do *immediately,* but since they only have a few seconds to do so, they pull out all the stops—and I mean *all*: illogical falsetto, misplaced scatting, and needless octave leaps. Pulling out a few stops is fine, but you have to keep some in your back pocket. You have to build. If you start at the top, there's nowhere left to go. It's crucial to keep the integrity of the song and not get lost in fancy runs. The artists I respect the most are the ones who can take a song and sing every note exactly as it was intended to be sung—no extra *ooh-ooh-oohs* or *whoa-ho-ho-hos* thrown in—and still be potent and heartfelt enough to make me weep.

Donnie Hathaway's version of Leon Russell's "A Song for You" and Bryan Adams's "Have You Ever Really Loved a Woman?" are two ideal examples of how, when you find the right mix of melody and meaning, you create the perfect love song. Those tunes taught me about not just love songs but love itself. Phil Stacey introduced me to the Adams tune, and the first time I heard him perform it, I went over and said, "I don't want you to take this in a weird or wrong way, but had I been the girl you were singing this to, my panties would've been on the stage." Phil is married and has two kids, and when he sings that song, you can tell that he's happy, and that he obviously knows what it's like to be in love. He broke down exactly what it means to be totally devoted to somebody without saying anything beyond what Bryan Adams wrote.

(Later that day, another hypertalented finalist named Gina Glocksen sang the same song, and she introduced it by saying, "I'd like to give a little disclaimer here: if you really want to know how to love a woman, you should probably listen to how Phil sung this." She then knocked it out of the park, after which I told her, "Okay, I almost went gay for Phil, but you got me back.")

Music also has the power to transcend time and place. Whenever I hear the soundtrack to the movie *Garden State*—which features awesome songs by the Shins, Colin Hay, Frou Frou, and a whole bunch of other moody, evocative artists—or the Postal Service album *Give Up*, no matter where I am or what I'm doing, I'm jetted right back to my freshman year of high school, sitting at a café, drinking an Italian vanilla soda.

Shyamali feels exactly the same way, so I wasn't surprised when, seemingly out of nowhere, she told me, "I'm going to be a singer-songwriter, and I'm going to travel the world, and teach the world what I know through my music. And this isn't something I want to do. This is something I *have* to do. This is where my life comes from. This is how I clarify."

I could relate.

I ended up singing in a gospel choir, which was led by an African-American woman, Pastor Pat Wright, and was comprised of a United Nations–like mix of races. The summer after my freshman year, we toured through Chicago, Nebraska, Oklahoma, Texas, and Mississippi, eventually arriving in New Orleans, where we helped with the post–Hurricane Katrina cleanup.

Our purpose was to spread hope and love through our music. We performed in a bunch of churches, but not as many as we'd planned for, because once in a while, when we rolled up in our bus filled with white people, and black people, and brown people, and yellow people, the closed-minded preacher would send us on our way. It made no sense. We were singing for hope, and that's a powerful thing, beyond race or faith.

Singing with the choir really opened my eyes to the power that spiritual music could have on even a confused spiritualist like me. "Swing Low, Sweet Chariot" was my big solo feature, and during a performance at one of the more backwater churches in Brownville, Nebraska, when I came to the lines "I'm sometimes up, and I'm sometimes down / Comin' for to carry me home / But still my soul feels heavenly bound / Comin' for to carry me home," I felt like I became a vessel of spiritual energy. Thanks to my singing, the music and good vibes flowed through the entire room, and everybody was able to focus and be happy.

If I had to identify my religion, it would have to be music. Singing is my version of praying; it's about meditation and performing for a higher purpose. I've been known to sit in my room and sing the same song—or even the same lick— over and over again, for hours on end. I used to practice singing along with Beyoncé's version of "Swing Low, Sweet Chariot," because I knew if I could come close to replicating that power and the feeling, well, that would give me some- thing to build on. At first, I wasn't focusing on singing the notes right, but rather on capturing that energy and concentrating it into the delivery. It's fun stuff when you get it right, a natural high. However, like all highs, this one doesn't last forever, so that means you have to buy more and more CDs to cop that melodic buzz. Music: it's my drug of choice.

I actually *have* to use music as my meditation, because when I try to meditate for real—when I try to shut off the noise in my brain and contemplate the world and my soul—I usually get distracted and end up going to the kitchen to get something to eat. But songs align my mind and enable me to think about things beyond the realm of normal conscious thought. Sometimes I get to the point where I feel like I can break down the meaning of life. (I would break it down for you right now, but that's a whole other book.) The basic idea is to do what makes you happy and compromise when needed.

Okay, that's barely a fraction of the whole thing, but we're talking about the meaning of life, so what do you expect?

Colors

In all of my grade schools, there were white kids, black kids, Asian kids, and me. We were all friends, and I never felt discriminated against, but the only brown people I could look up to on television were Aladdin and Mowgli.

I don't want it to sound like I had a hard, racism-filled childhood; I just noticed that when I was growing up, there were very few other Indian and Middle Eastern kids in my classes and in school. Every once in a while I would catch an odd look in the supermarket, or a snide comment on the street. But I just assumed that it was natural for someone with darker pigment to experience a little extra judgment here and there.

As it happened, when I was growing up in and around the

Seattle area, there wasn't too much overt racism, but there was plenty of discomfort. Most everybody was nice to me and Shyamali to our faces, but it was always easy to tell when somebody wasn't at ease talking to a brown person.

I have to explain why I use the word *brown* to describe myself or others with my skin tone. We're not black . . . although technically neither are black people. We're not white, though again, neither are white people. I'm Asian, but when people think Asian, they think Chinese, Japanese, or Korean. I've been called Mexican, Brazilian, black, Arabic, you name it, I've heard it. So I'm not saying brown in a discriminatory way, but rather brown as in not black or white. (And to make the color issue even more confusing, I'm also English, Irish, Dutch, and Italian. I'm a Eurasian mutt.)

I have a ten-year-old blond-haired, blue-eyed cousin who introduced Shyamali to one of her ten-year-old blond-haired, blue-eyed friends. A few days later, my cousin and her friend were hanging out in our living room, and from the kitchen, I heard my cousin mention something about Shyamali to the friend, and the friend said, "Oh, you mean that *colored* girl?"

I didn't know anybody even said "colored" anymore, let alone a ten-year-old kid. When my sister told me about it, I went up to my bedroom and thought about it for a while, and it boiled down to the question, *Where did a ten-year-old come up with "colored"?* The answer was simple: her parents. It's still disconcerting to realize that there are preteens running around the world pointing at Indian girls and calling them colored, just because their parents are stuck in the 1950s.

As you can imagine, 9/11 didn't help matters. At airports, I've had to deal with that whole you're-brown-so-you-must-be-a-terrorist thing numerous times. Let's get serious here: I'm a 125-pound teenager, traveling with my five-three, twenty-one-year-old sister. We were exactly what we looked like: Seattle metronational Bohemian Birkenstock wearers. We just happened to be brown.

I've never been able to discern a specific racist demographic. Some haters are young, some are old, some are men, and some are women. Fortunately, there are a lot of young people who have chosen to not make their parents' beliefs their own. They recognize the problems and they've opened their minds, and are trying to stop perpetuating the hate.

There are a lot of people in my generation who are interested in consciousness beyond consciousness, in thinking beyond thinking, in educating themselves beyond what they're taught in school, or what they read in magazines or see on television.

At my high school, there were a bunch of kids who went to school only because they had to. They'd be sitting at the back of the class, zoning out on what the teacher was saying, and drawing these incredible murals on their desks . . . which they'd have to wash off after the bell rang, because they knew if the teacher saw, they'd be in major trouble. Given their choice, they would have followed their heart and their art. As it was, they were branded troublemakers—at best tolerated, and at worst dismissed.

They shine. They're deep. I call them the Indigo Children.

These are children who are in touch with their intuition, their higher selves. They haven't had their natural sense of knowing taken away from them. They don't always fit into the norm. I was an Indigo Child. I still am. And I always will be.

Idol-ing Around

American *Idol* has become such a uniquely American phenomenon that people often forget it's not an American invention.

American Idol's predecessor was a UK show called *Pop Idol*, which was kind of a funky, glitzy, fan-friendly version of *Star Search*, the twist being that it was shown live, and the home audience decided who stayed and who went.

The series was created by a British guy named Simon— but not the Simon you might have guessed. Best known for having managed the Spice Girls, Simon Fuller came up with the idea for *Pop Idol* sometime around 2000. Fuller's format was pretty simple: Amateur and semiprofessional singers audition and perform for a panel of judges comprised of music industry heavyweights. The judges make their critiques, the fans take those critiques into account, then the home viewers phone in their votes. Each week, a contestant or two (or ten, or twenty-four) is eliminated until there's only one left. The winner is given a record deal, and all but guaranteed fame. However, fame's sister, fortune, isn't guaranteed, because if you win—or even if you finish in the Top 3—19 Management, the *Pop Idol* umbrella company, will own a chunk of your career for several years after you're off the show.

Pop Idol's most notorious judge was an A & R executive named Simon Cowell. *Idol* was the perfect forum for Cowell, who became known for his sarcastic putdowns of the wannabe stars. For example: "You sing like Mickey Mouse on helium." Sometimes, just for kicks, he'd dis singers even if they were really talented, but he was always so smart and funny about it that audiences loved him, even though they hated him.

Growing up, we didn't have a TV, so I was unaware of the phenomenon that was waiting to make its mark on popular culture. In 2001, all the major American networks wanted a reality show that would create as much excitement as *Survivor*. So as *Pop Idol* got bigger and bigger in England, the Simons—along with yet another Simonized UK producer named Simon Jones—went from network to network, pitching their Americanized version of *Pop Idol* . . . and nobody bit. Fox, the most risk-taking of the major networks, finally bought the show, which premiered in 2002.

The hosts for season one were a funny radio DJ named Ryan Seacrest and a comic named Brian Dunkleman, and there were three judges: Cowell, singer Paula Abdul (singer/dancer/choreographer of "Straight Up" fame), and a musician/record producer named Randy Jackson. From the get-go,

Simon was the sarcastic one, Paula was the sweet one, and Randy was the funky one. And also from the get-go, the show was *huge*.

I was in sixth grade when *American Idol* premiered, but it wasn't really on my radar. I had a friend who was an *Idol* freak, though, and since I was a singer, she thought I'd like it, so she dragged me into her basement and made me check it out. One of the first performers was a cute little brown-haired girl who was singing "(You Make Me Feel Like) A Natural Woman."

Both my friend and I were Mariah Carey fans—even today, Mariah is one of my main influences, and I sing along with her records to strengthen my falsetto. So we were blown away when this little girl hit the crazy, Mariah-like high note at the end of the chorus. My friend said, "OhMyGodShe's-AmazingI'mGoingToVoteForHerRightNow."

I said, "Um, yeah, she is pretty awesome. I'll vote for her too."

So we both cast our votes for the eventual season one winner, Kelly Clarkson.

(I should mention that I voted on *American Idol* on only three other occasions: once for Phil Stacey because he was awesome, once for Melinda Doolittle because she was amazing, and, just for the novelty of it, once for myself. And I really did vote for myself only that one time, because I felt it would be kind of lame if I stayed on the show because I stuffed the ballot box.)

Phil Stacey

I've spoken with folks from other Idol *seasons, and from what I can tell, I think our season was the first time that nobody was really out to win the competition. People were out there to have a great time, and we were very humbled by the experience. And all of us were surprised that we'd made it to that level. Everybody was very supportive to the point that we phoned in votes for each other. I voted for Jordin Sparks several times, and I threw a few votes Sanjaya's way too. It was a very positive environment.*

There wasn't ever a point in my life that I looked at my watch and thought, *Yay, it's eight o'clock! Time to watch* American Idol! But as a singer and a music fan, I felt it was important to check in on it once in a while, and I was generally glad I did. I didn't aspire to be Carrie Underwood or Ruben Studdard, but it was nice to see that regular people were given a chance to sing for millions of people.

After my freshman year of high school, we moved about a half hour north of Seattle so Mom could be with her boyfriend. He was an incredible guitar player who'd gone to the Berklee College of Music in Boston. He was the kind of guy who would buy, say, the new Rihanna CD not necessarily because he liked Rihanna, but so he could stay up on what was happening in the contemporary music scene. In that same vein, he watched and TiVo'd *American Idol* religiously, which made sense, because the person who won was guaranteed to have a well-produced album that was all but certain to go platinum . . . and you never knew if that person might need a guitar player. Occasionally, I'd sit down and watch it with him—this was season five, the year of Taylor Hicks, Chris Daughtry, Katharine McPhee, and Kellie Pickler—and my thinking about the whole thing was along the lines of, *That's cool that Taylor and Chris are getting up there and sing-*

ing, but I would neeeeeeevvvvver *do something like that. I would* neeeeeeevvvvver *go on a show like* American Idol. Neeeeeeevvvvver.

Part of my lack of desire to go on *Idol* had to do with where I grew up. Most of the Seattle music scene is indie and underground, and people thought going on *Idol* would be a totally sellout move . . . and honestly, I kind of did too. Which was why when a couple of friends from my gospel choir begged me to go on a road trip to Los Angeles to audition for the show, I said, "No. That's stupid. Why would I do that? Why would I sit in a stupid car with you guys for over twenty-four stupid hours just to try to be on some stupid show? I'm only a high school sophomore, and if I want to be a musician, I can do it anytime. I could start a band and sing at some bar in Seattle, and it would be fine. All *American Idol* does is create typical pop stars." I didn't ever want to be typical.

And I maintained that stance until I found out that the *Idol* people were holding auditions in Seattle.

Shyamali Malakar

People had been telling us for a long time that we should try out for American Idol. *I didn't want to do it, because if I was going to make it as a musician, I wanted to do it in a grassroots way, and I didn't want to be working with The Man, and there was that whole Seattle snob thing. It all kind of freaked me out. Sanjaya and Camilla had to work hard to convince me, saying, "Pleeeeeeeease, it's just downtown." Eventually I said okay. I figured there was a chance that something cool might happen.*

Doing Lines

Whether I liked it or not, the *Idol* seed had been planted, and as soon as I realized that I'd only need to go about twenty-four miles to audition instead of twenty-four hours, I thought, *What the hell. It'll be fun. I'll drag Shyamali and my cousin Camilla along, and we'll all give it a shot, and if it doesn't work out, I'll just go back to school, and things will go on like they always have.* So on September 19, 2006, the three of us did what everybody else who auditions for *American Idol* does: we woke up at the crack of dawn and stood in line for what felt like a zillion years.

The auditions were held at the Key Arena at Seattle Center, the big stadium just north of Seattle where they have all the professional basketball games and big rock concerts. At four in the morning, we went downtown hauling a big jug of throat-soothing honey-lemon-ginger tea that Mom had made for us, and we waited.

And waited.

And waited.

And waited.

Finally, at two in the afternoon, they started herding prospective contestants into the arena. And the *Idol* people kept yelling, "Make sure you have your two forms of ID in your hand! Two forms of ID. Not one. Two. Two forms of ID."

Oops.

I reached into my pocket and grabbed my wallet, which I knew contained exactly one form of ID, my Washington State ID card. So after ten hours of waiting, and after pouring down almost a gallon of honey-lemon-ginger tea, I'd be going home without even singing a note. That is, unless my mother made it down to the arena with my birth certificate within an hour.

Shyamali Malakar

We sat in the stadium for hours, and it was endless. I almost walked out on four different occasions.

While we were waiting for Mom, we heard periodic screams roll toward us from down the block. The noise kept getting closer and closer, and louder and louder . . . and then we realized that the crowd was roaring at the cameramen who were wheeling their equipment alongside the line. It was like everybody was doing a massive stadium wave, just so they could maybe get on TV for an eighth of a second. (At that point, the camera was a total novelty for me. I never thought for a minute that I'd get used to having one of them follow me around for almost twelve hours a day.)

Shyamali and Camilla both had all the identification they needed, so we kept heading toward the door as if nothing was wrong. When we got to the main entrance, Mom hadn't shown up, so we kept letting people go inside in front of us: "Go right ahead" . . . "No, please, we don't mind" . . . "Good luck" . . . "Don't worry about us, we'll be fine . . ."

The doors were about five minutes from closing when Mom ran over with the proper paperwork—but begrudgingly, because she hadn't wanted me there in the first place. "You're not ready," she'd told me the previous night. "And besides, you can do the show whenever you want. *American Idol* isn't going anywhere. Go to school for another year and get a little more mature, and see what happens next year."

I said, "What about Shyamali? She's young."

Mom said, "She's been working as a professional musician. She's closer to being ready. Do it next year."

"If I don't do it now, I'll probably never do it, because I'm not going far away to audition, and who knows if or when they'll ever come back to Seattle."

After another thirty minutes of debate, she threw up her hands and said, "Fine." Remember, I was a good debater.

Once we got inside the arena, the *American Idol* rep checked out our IDs, gave us each a piece of paper, and said, "See ya tomorrow!"

I said, "Um, tomorrow?"

She nodded. "Yep."

"Why?"

"Oh, today was just to give you your ticket to tell you where you'll be sitting in the arena tomorrow."

"Tomorrow?"

"Yep. Tomorrow."

"You mean I'm not singing for anybody?"

"Not unless you want to."

"So I waited here for almost twelve hours to get a piece of paper that tells me when I have to come back to wait some more tomorrow?"

"Yep."

"Just out of curiosity, what time are you guys here until tonight?"

"Eight."

"So I probably could've shown up at seven forty-five, and I would've been okay."

She shrugged. "Probably."

"So what sense did it make for us to get here at four in the morning?"

"Well, if you were the first person here, you'd be the first person to audition, and if you were the second person, you'd be the second, and so on."

"So does this mean I'll be one of the last people to audition tomorrow?"

"No, not *the* last. But you'll be waiting around for a while. So will we see you guys tomorrow?"

I sighed. "Yeah, I suppose."

The next day, Shyamali, Camilla, and I, jug of tea in hand, once again did hours upon hours of line waiting, but this time it was a bit more annoying than the previous day, because, in true Seattle fashion, it started to rain. (The rain didn't annoy me as much as some of the other singers, however, because as we know, I love precipitation.) While all of us bored hopefuls were trying to psychically open the arena's doors, the camera crew went up and down the sidewalk, filming B-roll sweeps of us getting drenched. (B-roll, by the way, is television talk for footage that will eventually be cut into a longer video segment, and a sweep is when they have a long, uncut shot of a big area—for instance, a bunch of people waiting in line, getting drenched.) When they ran this particular shot, they laid "Raindrops Keep Fallin' on My Head" underneath. Not *too* obvious, right?

When my little crew finally made it into the lobby, we were pulled aside by a cameraman, who asked me to say the phrase that I'd ultimately utter about four million times: "Hi, my name is Sanjaya Malakar, and I'm seventeen years old, and I'm from Seattle, Washington." Shyamali and Camilla followed suit, then we went off to audition.

There were twelve tables on the arena floor, which seated two *Idol* producers each. Every few minutes, a new group of four would strut up to one of the tables and take their turns singing. Then the producers would whisper to each other, scribble down some notes, and give the auditioners their verdict. Some of the people I heard singing were amazing, and others, not so much.

After five-plus hours of hanging out, our foursome—me, Shyamali, Camilla, and some random girl—were invited to do our thing. The producer, who looked like a sexy librarian, what with her cute glasses and her long, wavy red-blond hair, smiled at me and said, "What's your name, how old are you, and where are you from?"

I said the magical line: "My name is Sanjaya Malakar, and I'm seventeen years old, and I'm from Seattle, Washington."

The other producer, who was equally pretty but way less librarianish and way funkier, asked, "And what will you be singing for us today?"

" 'Swing Low, Sweet Chariot.' "

I took a deep breath and cranked out my favorite spiritual as best I could. I never moved all that much when I sang "Swing Low" with my gospel choir—there's only so much moving you can do in a choir—and that day was no different. That I was unbelievably nervous didn't exactly help matters. After I finished, the sexy librarian nodded and said, "Hmm, that was great, Sanjaya. But remember, this is a TV show, and you need to be entertaining. Maybe you should sing something a little more up-tempo. And maybe give us more energy."

Some of the singers who were auditioning probably got upset when the producers gave them direction, but I wasn't the least bit offended. The producers had probably been doing this for a long time, and they undoubtedly knew what they were talking about. Plus they were totally chill, and they didn't make me feel as if I was being steamrolled. I said, "Okay. I'll do 'Signed, Sealed, Delivered.' " I knew that song backward and forward, so I was able to get into it and actually enjoy performing it.

After I zipped through the tune, the sexy librarian smiled and said, "Great, great, that was a lot better. You can go through." She gestured toward my sister and said, "Your turn."

Shyamali went up there and absolutely crushed Norah Jones's "Don't Know Why," but the sexy librarian said, "Hmm, that was great, but how about something more up-tempo?"

I yelled out, *"Pussycat Dolls!"*

Shyamali smiled and said, "Sure, I'll do a Pussycat Dolls

tune." Which she also crushed. It was no surprise that they let her through too.

Next up was Camilla. She said, "I'm going to sing Herbie Hancock's 'A Song for You.'" That's a tune Herbie recorded with Christina Aguilera, and Camilla had it down cold. She added in all of Christina's vocal leaps and bounds, as well as some of her own, and it was incredible. Every note was perfect, because that's how Camilla rolls.

Unfortunately, she sang without moving, just like I did, but unlike with me, they wouldn't give her a second chance. My guess is that they didn't want her because although she was beautiful, she was also a white girl, and they probably already had reached their beautiful-white-girl quota. It also might've helped if she'd gotten more into the performance.

Shyamali Malakar

I think that the producers already have an idea of what they're looking for, so in some cases, even if you're really good—like Camilla—but don't fit their mold, they don't want you. But the further I got into the process, the cooler it got, partly because I started feeling validated.

There's also the possibility that they were turned off by the fact that Camilla did too many Christina-ish runs. Sometimes if you go overboard with that kind of thing, you lose the integrity of the song. (Chris Richardson, one of the *Idol* finalists from my season, has the best control of any vocalist I've ever heard. He can do things with his voice that are beyond comprehension. But he sometimes gets insecure and will feel the need to seek everybody's approval, so every now and then, he'll try to do a bit too much. It's understandable why—if he has the ability to do those kinds of spectacular runs, why not put them out there once in a while?—but sometimes he'd go somewhat overboard.)

If you serve the music, the music will serve you.

The Good, the Bad, the Ugly, and the Really Ugly

Some of the singers that made it to the next level were obviously untalented, while some that didn't make it were brilliant, Camilla being a prime example. It got to the point where it was impossible to guess who the producers would or wouldn't approve. There was the girl I fell into a conversation with who told me that she didn't know what she was going to sing. "I'm just gonna go in there and do what I feel right at that moment."

I said, "You don't have anything planned?"

"Nope. Nothing."

"Ummmmm, okay. Hope that works out for you." I knew there was no way she'd make it. You have to prepare at least somewhat.

She ended up singing a Christina Aguilera ballad, one of the ones with the crazy runs, the high high notes, the low low notes, and every note in between. She tried to sing it exactly like Christina. Now, Camilla could get away with that sort of thing, because she's astounding. But this girl, well, suffice it to say that when she went to the next level of auditions—yes, they let her through—I knew she'd better prepare herself to take some serious criticism from the *Idol* folks. (Sometimes you'd get called out not on your performance but on your choice of material. I was even zinged a couple of times for taking on some of Stevie Wonder's more difficult material. But I managed to get away with it, because I'd been singing Stevie's music for my entire life; I knew what he was about, and it helps to get inside the tune, which enabled me to perform it in a way that makes people recognize I kind of know what I'm doing.)

All the people that you see on *Idol* who can't sing in the least had to make it through not one, not two, but three auditions before they sang for Simon, Randy, and Paula. I grew to suspect that folks in charge of choosing who do and don't make it are clearly told, "Put everybody in two groups: the good ones and the bad ones. Pick the best of the good ones based on production value. Pick the worst of the bad ones based on entertainment value." From the first time we saw that process at the Key Arena, Shyamali and I felt horrible about the fact that these poor people were being jerked around and made fun of just so viewers would tune in. We hated seeing people fooled into believing they'd be able to realize an impossible dream, only to be insulted a few weeks later on one of the most-watched TV shows in the world. Unfortunately ratings would go down if they eliminated the practice altogether.

The Final Hurdle

We went home after the cattle call and waited to get our contracts. Two months later, we went to the next set of auditions at the W Hotel in downtown Seattle. Almost immediately after we got to the waiting area, a cameraman shoved a camera into my face, asked me to introduce myself ("My name is Sanjaya Malakar, and I'm seventeen years old, and I'm from Seattle, Washington"), then told me to give my story. "Well, my sister is here auditioning with me, and I just got out of high school, and I want to be a singer because I love singing, and I want to be on *American Idol* because it looks like a lot of fun." I sounded horrible, and unpolished, and dorky.

At this set of auditions, there was this cute, curvy little

singer from Phoenix who seemed to be singing in front of my sister at every stop. It was tough for Shaymali, because she's a jazzy, loungy singer, and this girl was a flat-out powerhouse R & B goddess. Having to follow that constantly was awkward and difficult, but how could you get mad at Jordin Sparks?

Jordin was far more experienced, and far better trained than any of us. She'd been on *Star Search* and *America's Most Talented Kids*, but she wasn't the least bit affected. She told us that she'd auditioned for *American Idol* in San Diego, and the judge said to her, "You're amazing! You're awesome! And you should go audition in another city!"

Jordin said, "What?! Why don't you just put me through? Why do I have to go through this whole mess again?"

"We just think it would be for the best."

"Why?"

They repeated, "We just think it would be for the best."

To this day, I don't know if Jordin knows why she had to audition twice. I certainly don't. Then she went off and won a competition in her home state called *Arizona Idol*, after which she was sent to Seattle and given a "golden ticket," which enabled her to blow off a lot of the hoops that the rest of us had to jump through, and go on to California. But she still had to perform for the cameras in Seattle, so she sang her song. After she got through, Shyamali did her thing, and after she got through, I got really, really, really, really nervous, because I couldn't imagine that they'd take all three of us from our little group.

Jordin Sparks

Sanjaya was the first Idol person I met, and I knew right away that he was the kind of person I'd be friends with. Plus he was crazy, so I knew we'd be able to talk. He was kind of shy, but I could tell that he'd be outgoing once you got to know him. But once he comes out of his shell, well, sometimes you want to put him back in. We started talking music, and I found out that he has really eclectic tastes. I thought I was all over the map, but he was talking about people I had no idea about.

So I trudged into the audition room and said, "My name is Sanjaya Malakar, and I'm seventeen years old, and I'm from Seattle, Washington, and I'm going to sing 'I'll Make Love to You' by Boyz II Men."

The artist manager—there weren't judges at this point, just "artist managers"—gave me a once-over, most likely thinking, *This scrawny, awkward, nervous kid is going to tell me about how he'll make love to me? Ooooooohhhhkay.* When I started singing, he gave me a look that I read as *This kid doesn't have it.*

After I finished, he walked around the table, put his hand on my shoulder, and said, "You're a really good singer, but you should go home and practice. You're not ready for the show. You don't make the cut."

While I wandered back into the waiting area, somewhat dazed and mildly bummed out, I thought, *Okay, that sucked, but whatever. My sister made it, and that's cool enough. I'll hang out for the rest of the day and support her.*

Shyamali's next stop was a performance for *Idol* executive producers Ken Warwick and Nigel Lythgoe, and while I waited out in the hallway, she wowed them.

"You did great," Ken said. "I guess that means tougher competition for your brother."

She said, "Um, my brother got cut."

Nigel said, *"What?!"* He then grabbed his walkie-talkie and started screaming at some poor production assistant in an unintelligible English accent. A couple minutes later, Shyamali poked her head out the door and said, "Um, they want you in there."

I pointed at my chest. "What? Me?"

"Yes. You." She walked over and kissed me on the cheek. "I think you're in."

I was stunned. I'd already been cut, and my guard was down, and I was feeling relaxed because I knew I wouldn't have to do anything for the rest of the day other than support Shyamali. I said, "Oh, man, okay, here goes," then took a deep breath and headed into the room.

Ken smiled at me and asked, "So who are you?"

On autopilot, I said, "My name is Sanjaya Malakar, and I'm seventeen years old, and I'm from Seattle, Washington."

Nigel asked, "What song did you sing before you got cut?"

"Um . . . er . . . um . . . uh . . . er . . . um . . ." I couldn't remember the damn song. All I kept thinking was, *Why am I even in this room?*

Ken said slowly, as if speaking to a toddler, "You sang Boyz II Men, right? 'I'll Make Love to You,' wasn't it?"

I said, "Right, right, right, right."

Nigel said, "Right."

I said, "Right."

Ken said, "Right. How about you sing that for us?"

I said, "Right." As I ran down the tune, I made a conscious effort to not be nervous, to be relaxed. Unfortunately, I couldn't calm my nerves, and now I was confused to boot, so

I'm sure I wasn't particularly convincing when I told every-body in the room that I'd make love to them, like I always did, and that I'd hold them tight, all through the night.

Nigel said, "Um, okay, Sanjaya, you're a really good singer, but that might not be the best material for you. How about you try 'Don't Cha' by the Pussycat Dolls?"

I said, "You want me to do a Pussycat Dolls song to see if I know how to sing?" They're cool, but "Don't Cha" isn't the best barometer to judge somebody's vocal skills.

Ken said, "Right."

"Not, like, Stevie Wonder or something?"

"Nope. Pussycat Dolls."

"All right." So I musically asked the judges if they wished their girlfriends were hot like me, which didn't make me feel any less awkward about the situation.

They were silent for almost a full minute after I finished. Finally, Nigel stood up, walked over, put his hand on my shoulder, and said, "You're a decent singer, but you need to be more confident . . ."

My heart sank. Shyamali was wrong. I was done. I'd wasted my time.

" . . . but we're putting you through."

After Shyamali, Jordin, and I had a little group hug, I thought about what Ken and Nigel had said. They were right: I was a decent singer, and I needed more confidence, and wasn't anywhere near as talented as, say, Jordin. But I had two things on my side that a lot of other *Idol* hopefuls didn't have: brown skin, and a sister who was already on the show.

We were stoked. I mean, how could we not be? We were Shyamali and Sanjaya Malakar, the brother-sister duo that was going to take over *American Idol*.

How <small>simon</small> Became SIMON

One of the things I'm asked the most often is "Is Simon Cowell really that mean?" Talk about a loaded question. If I say yes, some might accuse me of sour grapes, and if I say no, I could come across as cavalier. The thing is, what with all of his sarcastic comments, his movie-star persona, and his guest shots on shows like *Family Guy* and *The Simpsons*, people sometimes forget that Simon Cowell is one of the most powerful figures not just in television and music but in all of entertainment.

His father was an executive at EMI Music Publishing in England, but Simon wasn't handed anything on a silver platter. Okay, that's not *exactly* true: after Simon dropped out of college, his dad got him a job at EMI . . . but it was in the mail room. It wasn't like Simon's dad said, "Okay, son, you've quit school, and you don't work well with others, and you have no experience, so here's your corner office and six-figure salary." No, Simon started in the industry on the ground floor, figured out how to do a variety of jobs well, and clawed his way up. You have to respect that.

Either because he was bored with publishing or because a strong sense of ambition came to life, Simon left EMI and started up a music company called E&S Music, which pretty much tanked, and in 1989, he was forced to declare bankruptcy and move back in with his parents. That couldn't have been fun for a guy who was about to turn thirty; I got my own place when I was eighteen, and while I love my mother, I don't think I'll be living with her again anytime soon.

The next year, Simon picked himself up, dusted himself off, and went to work at an indie record label called Fanfare Records. Fanfare had a handful of huge hits in the UK, none of which made any significant noise in the United States. Fanfare eventually got sucked up by BMG, who hired Simon as an A & R consultant and gave him his own little label, which he dubbed S Records. S signed and nurtured such acts as Curiosity Killed the Cat, Ultimate Kaos, and Westlife. These artists were million-sellers in their homeland, but never had any notable success overseas.

Simon generated a ton of money over the intervening years, and everybody who knew him figured he'd get huge at some point, but nobody could have anticipated the *Pop Idol* and *American Idol* juggernaut. Who would have guessed that the Kelly Clarksons, the Carrie Underwoods, the Clay Aikens, the Daughtrys, and even the William Hungs of the world would become cash cows for Simon and the *Idol* management company, 19 Entertainment? Who would have guessed that Simon would create other reality television hits, including such music-themed shows as *America's Got Talent*, *Celebrity Duets*, and *Grease: You're the One That I Want!* Who would have guessed that he would develop the power to give an unknown, inexperienced, skinny little singer from Seattle the chance at a music career?

This, of course, was why I was trembling like a tuning fork the first time I sang for Simon Cowell.

The Big Three and Me

I tried to stay chill before my October 14 appearance in front of Simon, Randy, and Paula—an appearance that, if it went well, would get me through to *American Idol*'s legendary Hollywood Week—but it was tough. Yes, I wasn't as much of an *Idol* fanatic as most of the other prospective contestants were, so I was probably a little bit less starstruck than the majority of the crowd, but how could I not be nervous? Even though my only semiprofessional experience in the music industry was with my gospel choir, and even though I didn't watch all that much television, I was well aware that Simon was about as big as it got.

This is probably a good time to point out that singing is a lot harder than it looks. Sure, you can sing and be powerful, hit the right notes and add in some emotion, and it some-times comes out sounding cool. But that's hard enough to do when you have proper singing technique. Thing is, at that point, I didn't sing correctly at all. I sung from my throat, which you're not supposed to do. I sounded okay, and people told me "You sound great," but anybody who knows technique knew I wasn't singing properly. I'd never had any consistent formal training—since we moved around a lot, it was difficult to establish a relationship with a vocal coach—but I did enough musical theater to develop chops and stamina, which is something that not everybody has. So I had some pluses and some minuses, all of which the judges would be able to spot easily.

By the time Shyamali and I went to do our thing in front of the Big Three, Simon, Paula, and Randy had been through five seasons of *Idol* and had listened to literally thousands of singers, if not tens of thousands, some of whom were as unbe-lievably awesome as Ms. Underwood, and some of whom were as scary bad as Mr. Hung. Shyamali and I knew we were some-where in between, so we were a little freaked out about how we'd be received by the judges. But at least we had each other around for support—as well as our father and a bunch of our friends—so that made the whole thing a little bit easier.

Clothingwise, I decided to go with an outfit that I'd origi-nally planned to wear for a show with my gospel choir: a shiny cream-colored short-sleeved button-down shirt with a tan collar and matching tan pants.

(I'd actually also worn this for my first audition with the producers in Seattle, so I had no choice but to take it with me for the Big Three, because whatever you wear at the begin-ning, you have to wear at the end, just in case they need to edit something together to make it look like one big audition.

It's worth mentioning that sometimes the editors will completely mess with the chronology. Gina Glocksen, one of the finalists from my season, told me that her Simon-Randy-Paula audition that made it onto the show was actually her producer audition. They edited the judges' comments around her performance from several months before, and they did such a great job that I never in a million years would've guessed it had Gina not said anything.)

Melinda Doolittle

One of my friends told me before my first appearance, "Don't forget, first and foremost, it's a television show." And you hear that, and you understand that, but you don't fully grasp it until you've been through the experience. We sometimes had to reshoot real events so many times that they stopped being real at all.

After we were given ID numbers to pin on our shirts—Shyamali was 80202 and I was 80203—the producers pulled us aside for an interview. After we got all of the biographical stuff out of the way, the interviewer asked us whether we'd be auditioning together or separately. I said, "We could sing together, but I think it would be more fun to compete against each other."

The producer smiled and said, "Can we get more about your sibling rivalry?"

I said, "Ummmmmmm, we don't really have that much of a sibling rivalry."

"Well, pretend. Maybe you could even get a little bit physical." He pointed at Shyamali and said, "Maybe you could push him or something."

Shyamali said, "Okay, here goes." She took a deep breath, looked into the camera, and boasted, "Whether or not he thinks he's going to make it, I'm going to make it further. Because he wouldn't even be this far if it wasn't for me."

That actually was true, so I nodded and said "Yeah," and then added, "but that's what *she* thinks. We all know that I'm the next American Idol."

"He's confident," Shyamali said. "Confident but foolish."

I said, "I'm cooler."

"But cooler doesn't cut it." (The bickering felt quite natural, because we're loud Italians, and loud Italians are great at bickering with their families.) She paused, then asked the producer, "Do you want me to push him now?" And sure enough, she pushed me. She hadn't pushed me since I was, like, ten. The funny thing is that they were trying to get us to look like sibling rivals, but we ended up coming across as really close.

A few minutes after we finished up the interview, Ryan Seacrest wandered over and asked me, "So are you guys related?"

Ryan seemed like the kind of guy you could mess with, so I said, "No. We just met here in line."

"You are related," he said. "You have to be."

I almost asked him what he meant by "have to be," but I just repeated, "Nope. We met in line."

Ryan smiled and said, "You mean in line at the hospital?" We all laughed, then he wandered off to harass another auditioner.

Finally it was Shyamali's turn to go in, and as my sister

strutted up to the stage, Paula completely botched her name. "Okay," she said, "Shy-uh-molly, shy-molly . . . shy . . ."

My sister walked out onto the stage and very sweetly said, "It's *Shah*-muh-lee."

Randy teased, "Yeah, I got it right the first time."

Paula, looking very put together and perfectly coiffed, rolled her eyes and said, "Tell us who you are."

"Hi"—she smiled—"my name is Shyamali Malakar, and I'm from Seattle, and I'm nineteen years old, and I'm going to sing 'Summertime,' a nice standard jazz classic." From out in the waiting area, I gave her a mental round of applause, because I love the way she does "Summertime."

Phil Stacey

You could tell that Sanjaya and Shyamali were really cheering each other on, and he was very upset when she got eliminated. I think Sanjaya would've been just as happy if she made it through and he didn't.

I thought she nailed it, and Paula kind of agreed. "You seem very nervous, and you don't have reason to be. You're very good. Very subtle, but great. You have a great energy. I think your voice is great."

Shyamali kind of giggled and said, "Thanks."

But then Paula turned to her left and unleashed the tiger. "What do you think, Simon?"

Simon, looking tired but handsome, clad as usual in a

tight T-shirt, shook his head and said, "Nothing unique. Nothing different. Very pretty, but nothing unusual."

Paula rolled her eyes and told my sister, "I like you . . ."

Randy, who was wearing the coolest designer glasses ever, and a strangely patterned blue button-down shirt with a white collar, interrupted Paula. "And I like you too, but I still think you have to find out who you are, and where you should fit. You've got a good voice."

Paula said to Simon, "Guess what? You just heard two yesses."

Now it was Simon's turn to roll his eyes. He told Shyamali, "I'm not jumping out of my chair, but Squiddley and Diddley over here said yes."

Shyamali gave the judges a cockeyed grin. "I'd be shocked if you jumped out of your chair, Simon."

Randy and Paula cracked up and clapped, then Randy pointed at Shyamali and said, "Whoaaaaaaaaaaa, *that's* the attitude I want."

Paula said, "Yeah, you need to bring that attitude to Hollywood. Congratulations, sweetheart. But you're going to work on your showmanship . . ."

Then Randy said, ". . . and your songs . . ."

Then Paula said, ". . . and your repertoire . . ."

Then Randy said, ". . . and your dynamics . . ."

Then Simon said, "So I guess she needs to change everything, yeah?"

Paula smirked at Simon, then smiled at Shyamali and sweetly said, "Get outta here."

As I was getting ready to go into the room, Ryan came over, pointed at me, and said, "Your mom tells me that you're the better singer, but you don't have the confidence . . ."

Right then, Shyamali burst through the door, arms raised above her head, jumping and screaming and yelling. Ryan cocked his thumb at her and said, ". . . however, she made it through." She ran right into Dad's arms, and after she got many pats on the back from our crew, Ryan caught her eye, pointed at me, and said, "Give your sister a hug." After a two-second, too-quick embrace, Ryan said, "Hey, brother, good luck. You're up."

So in I went. I was in a good space, because Shyamali got through. Even if I didn't make it, at least my sister did, and it was all good.

When I got onto the stage, I gave myself a quick pep talk: *Okay, this isn't bullshit anymore. You got cut and they brought you back, so you have to bring it.* So I tried to act like I owned the place. I yelled out *the* line: "*Hi, my name is Sanjaya Malakar, and I'm seventeen years old, and I'm from Seattle.*"

Randy seemed taken aback. "Oh. Okay. Well, hello, Sanjaya Malakar, what're you going to sing for us?"

"*I'm going to sing 'Swing Low, Sweet Chariot.'*"

In gospel choir, we did this thing that we liked to call the Gospel Rock, which is simply swaying from one foot to the other on beats two and four. So I swayed and sang, and two verses and one chorus later, Paula said, "Great, Sanjaya." (She pronounced my name correctly, by the way.) "You're a really good singer."

Randy said, "Yeah. You are." Then he looked me right in the eye and said, "Your sister just made it through. Are you better than her?"

I thought about it for a second. Shyamali's voice was so beautiful, and she was always confident and relaxed, and she had a *thing*. I didn't have a *thing* yet, so I said, "I don't think so."

Randy paused, then said, "At least you're being honest."

Paula, who was even tinier in real life than on television, so tiny that I wanted to put her in my pocket and take her home with me, asked, "You're the shy one of the two of you?" I nodded. "I don't know, I think your sister was a little bit more shy than you." I'd said about three words to them, so I wasn't sure how she came up with that.

Randy asked, "So you're inspired by Stevie Wonder?"

I mumbled, "Yeah."

Paula perked up. "Oh, great. Why don't you sing some Stevie for us?"

So I launched into "Signed, Sealed, Delivered." As I Gospel Rocked my way through the first verse, Paula bopped her head back and forth, and even let out a little "woo." Randy folded his arms and carefully examined me as if I were a lab experiment. And from my angle, Simon looked like he was doing everything in his power to stay awake, but he barely succeeded. (Outside of the live show, Simon *always* looked tired.)

Before I even got to the chorus, Simon very patronizingly said, "Okay, okay," as if it would've been physically painful for him to listen to the rest of the song.

Paula, bless her heart, clapped three times and quietly said, "Yay."

Randy leaned forward and asked Simon, "So what did you think of Sanjaya?"

Simon raised his eyebrows and told Randy, "He's a lot better than his sister . . ."

Randy nodded. "I think so too. Wow. Crazy."

Simon continued, ". . . because she has the stage presence, but he has the better voice." He turned to me and said, "You're like this shy little thing who's got *the* voice." Being the shy little thing, I couldn't think of anything interesting to say, but I was beyond thrilled that I'd gotten Simon Cowell's approval. He's not just a producer, he's a music CEO, and when you're auditioning, you're in his office. And if you're wasting his time, he's going to tell you in no uncertain terms, and you know what? That's okay, because it's his office.

Randy asked the panel, "So Paula? Simon? Yes? Yes?" They both nodded and applauded. "You heard it, Sanjaya. You're going to Hollywood! You da bomb! Work it out, baby!"

Melinda Doolittle

There was this buzz about Sanjaya's and Shyamali's singing, and how wonderful they both were. Then one day I saw this little guy, and he's the cutest thing, just precious and sweet. I won-dered, Is he going to be in this? Is he coming with us? When I first heard him, I thought, This dude is good.

Right outside the door, Shyamali heard Randy hooting and hollering, and told Dad and our posse of relatives, "Wow. I think they liked him better than they liked me."

Ryan asked her, "You think? Is that possible?"

But before Ryan could cause any more trouble, I shoved the door open, wearing the hugest smile ever. Everybody knew before I even said a word that I'd made it to Hollywood Week.

After Shyamali and I had a celebratory hug, Ryan put a hand on my shoulder and said, "I just have one question." He gestured at the audition room. "Who do they think is the better singer?"

I didn't know how to handle that one, so I took the Fifth Amendment. "Um . . . um . . . um . . . I'm not going to say."

I was finally starting to truly enjoy my *Idol* experience. I went from ambivalence to excitement, and I'd only been ambivalent in the first place because I was new to all this. At first, the way I saw it, *American Idol* was a show where some people sang really well, and some people sang really badly, and the bad ones got cut immediately, and the good ones got cut one by one, and Simon made fun of some of them, and eventually somebody won. Once I became part of the machine, once I stood in front of Simon, Paula, and Randy, once I bonded with the first TV people I'd ever met other than a local Seattle newscaster, it hit me that this was real. But not just real:

REAL.

General Education

One of the *American Idol* rules is that all contestants have to either be enrolled in high school or have a high school diploma by the time of Hollywood Week. I was in the middle of my sophomore year, and considering my performance in my freshman year, there was no way I was graduating early.

Which meant I had to take a GED test. And pass it. And get the paperwork to the *Idol* home office immediately.

I barely had a chance to prepare—I got the GED study book only three days before the test—but I still felt good about my chances. Why, I don't know, but I did. The first part of the test was math, science, and reading comprehension.

Part two of the test, the essay portion, was scheduled for the following day, but there was a massive snowstorm, so it got canceled, and Mom had to call the *Idol* people and beg them for extra time. "He took half of the test," Mom told the producer, "and he passed it with flying colors." (We had no idea if I'd passed, but it sounded good.) "Now all the schools are closed, and we're stuck."

From all the way on the other side of the room, I could hear the producer screaming at my mother: "*Ahhhhhhh! He can't go on the show without it! Ahhhhhhh!*"

The next week, the roads were clear enough that I was able to get to the school to write the essay that, if I nailed it, would give me the opportunity to be the one, the only American Idol.

The essay question was the most apt essay question in the history of essay questions: "Explain Why You Think That Television Can Be Beneficial."

My first thought was, *If this is the question to determine whether you can get a high school diploma without actually going to high school, then something is seriously wrong with the system.* And my second thought was, *I'm about to be on television, and I'm certain that no matter what happens, it's going to be a beneficial experience.*

But I didn't think it would be a wise idea to discuss *Idol*, so I took a more preachy path: "Networks such as Food TV and the Discovery Channel, when viewed in moderation, can be of great benefit to a young person, because it is almost as if they are going to school and being entertained at the same time. There are plenty of other things about television that blah-blah-blah-blah-blah."

An essay question about television when I was about

to be on television? Talk about a sign that I was making the right move.

(P.S.: There was another major snowstorm the day after I wrote my television-is-beneficial essay, and had I missed the test that day, I would've missed the *Idol* deadline. Cosmic, very cosmic . . .)

Pre-Hollywood Holidays

Before Hollywood Week, we went home to celebrate Christmas, which, in true Italian fashion, was a mind-blowing feast. As usual, a million aunts, uncles, and cousins, as well as a good number of their friends, showed up at my aunt Kathy's house. (Okay, there weren't a million people—it was more like fifty—but it felt like a million.) All the invites brought at least one dish, and there was enough food to feed practically everybody who'd auditioned at the Key Arena.

At most holidays, when we'd show up, Shyamali would make a beeline to Amber, our cousin who was closest to her in age; to that end, I always gravitated toward Camilla, Makenzie, and Melissa. This year, however, I couldn't even find

Camilla, because the second we opened the door, we were attacked:

"*Ohmigawd, tell us about the audition!*"

"*Ohmigawd, what did Simon say?*"

"*Ohmigawd, when're you leaving for Hollywood Week?*"

"*Ohmigawd, can I take a picture of you?*"

"*Ohmigawd, can I have your autograph?*"

"*Ohmigawd, ohmigawd, ohmigawd!*"

All of a sudden, we *were* the party, and it completely freaked me out. I tried to be polite, and answer everybody's questions, but all I wanted to do was find Camilla and go hide in one of the bedrooms. The concept of autographing stuff for my family was incomprehensible. It was like the Beatles in *A Hard Day's Night*. People that John, Paul, George, and Ringo had known for their entire lives were suddenly just like every other Beatlemaniac; they wanted a piece of them. But it wasn't *them* they wanted a piece of; they wanted to be hanging out with a *Beatle*. Not Richard Starkey, the good son or uncle or cousin, but Ringo Starr, the international superstar drummer. And to some extent, that's how it was that Christmas. It wasn't like, "Oh, cool, Sanjaya and Shaymali are here. We love our nephew and niece." It was, "*Ahhhhhhhh, the Malakars are on* American Idol! *Let's talk to them about the show, and absolutely nothing else!*"

But then there was the other faction of the family who weren't all that impressed and had an opinion about *everything*—and they weren't scared to share it with anyone and everyone, so naturally they opened up the floor for discussion. One of my uncles asked, "Show of hands. Who here thought they could really do it?" Most everybody threw their arms up in the air, and my uncle said, "Yeah, right. I'm sure the second you guys heard about it, most of you thought, *No way.* I, on the other hand, have believed in them the whole time." It went on in that vein for most of dinner and was all very dramatic, but Italians love drama, so I shouldn't have been surprised. Actually, I thought it was cool, because I believe that leaving it all out on the table is healthy, so I just listened.

It was weird hearing my family break it down and get all giddy. If it was my friends at school doing the breaking down, that would've made more sense—ironically, my school friends were very blasé about the whole thing—but these were people who have pictures of me running through sprinklers in my underwear. They shouldn't have wanted or needed shots of me giving them the Fan Smile.

(I used to think that I had two smiles, one that was a natural reaction smile, and one that was a "Fan Smile." Although I have multiple smiles, they all come from the heart.)

If things were this weird with the family at this point, I could only imagine what would happen once our shows were actually aired in January.

Hooray for Hollywood, That Screwy, Ballyhooed Hollywood

Right after New Year's, it was off to California for Hollywood Week.

Hollywood Week is *American Idol*'s version of boot camp. They take five days out of your life and put you in as many performance and audition situations as they can. The ultimate goal is to break down the *Idol* hopefuls until they're one big, open, raw nerve. On one hand, it seems kind of sadistic—but on the other hand, it makes sense to see if we can handle long hours and intense pressure, because if you win *Idol*, the time and pressure crunches become insane. I suppose they figure that if you can handle Hollywood Week, you can simultaneously handle a sixty-shows-in-fifty-days tour, and daily local television appearances, and ten phone interviews in one day, and post-gig meet-and-greets, and early-morning in-store appearances, and weekly trips to the studio so you can overdub the three words in the second verse that the producer wasn't happy with.

During Hollywood Week, you lose all sense of the outside world. You're able to call friends and family, but you rarely do, because during the day, they have you running from locale to locale, and at night, you're too exhausted to do anything but sleep.

Shyamali, Mom, and I flew into LAX from Seattle—Mom had to be with me because I was under eighteen—and we were instructed that when we made it down to baggage claim, we were supposed to look for somebody in a uniform holding a sign that said CLAY, which was the secret code for "Yo, *American Idol* people, follow me."

We tracked down the CLAY guy, and I asked him, "Are you here for *American Idol?*"

He shushed me, then mumbled out of the corner of his mouth, "Yes." The guy acted like a Secret Service agent.

I said, "*Cool!* What happens next?"

He shushed me again, then said, "Wait here."

So we waited, and slowly but surely, my fellow *Idol* wannabes started trickling in. I wanted to introduce myself and make some friends, but then I thought, *This is my competition. Better keep a low profile for right now.* For the most part, I huddled with my sister, but if somebody looked particularly cool, I wandered over and said hey.

Shyamali and I ended up hanging out with a singer who

would eventually become one of my closest friends on the show, Phil Stacey. I said, "Wouldn't it be amazing if we all ended up in the Top Twenty-four?" Little did we know.

Phil Stacey

I'm one of those guys who kind of sticks to themselves, and I'm usually shy around new people, but I clicked with Sanjaya right away. He had a fresh excitement about him, and I could tell he was happy to be there. He was the first contestant who I met in Hollywood, and he, Shyamali, and their mother were very friendly and welcoming, and they were fun to be around. A lot of people who made it to the Top 10 became friends right away during Hollywood Week. For instance, Chris Richardson and Blake Lewis bonded immediately, and Gina Glocksen and Haley Scarnato got really tight, and Jordin Sparks and Melinda Doolittle were inseparable, and I ended up rooming with Chris Sligh. By the time we made it into the Top 24, we felt that it was almost like we were all meant to be there together.

There were about 175 *Idol* hopefuls who'd been invited to Hollywood Week, the vast majority of whom were girls. After we got settled into the hotel, they divided us up by gender; the girls stayed around to audition, and we boys went on a field trip to Redondo Beach. One of the male contestants was an Oklahoman who had never seen the ocean, and when we hit the beach he freaked out, because it came crashing down on him just how big the world is. He was close to crying. As I watched him looking at the water, I realized how lucky I was that I'd grown up where I'd grown up, and that I'd seen what I'd seen.

Jordin Sparks

I looked around the bus and thought, Wow, I might actually be with these people for a while. And when it ended up happening, I thought, Ooooooookkkkaaayyyy, this is weird. Like that first day, I complimented LaKisha Jones on her necklace, and we started talking, and we became friends, and then we were in the Top 4 together. Karma! But both Sanjaya and I believe that everything happens for a reason, so I guess I shouldn't have been that surprised.

We were then taken to Venice Beach, where we were treated to the sight of its iconic thong-wearing musclemen. We went to an outdoor gym and had our fellow contestants snap photos of us pretending to work out. Then they organized us by rows for a group shot, with one of the thong guys right up front. Just as the photographer counted us down—"Three . . . two . . . one . . . smile!"—Thong Guy bent over and flexed every muscle in his body, so in the picture, everybody within spitting distance of him is grimacing, covering their eyes, or looking away from his bethonged butt. (I was way in the back, so I avoided seeing the Venice Beach moon. I wasn't scarred.)

We were treated as minor celebrities by the beachgoers,

not because anybody out in the real world knew what we were about to do, but because we were traveling in a group that was being trailed by cameras. On our way back to the bus after we finished up at the beach, a girl wandered over and asked me, "Who're all you guys?"

I calmly said, "We're with *American Idol*."

The girl squealed, "*Coooooool!* Hopefully we'll see you later in the season!"

"Yeah," I said. "Hopefully."

(Our day around L.A. was a blast, but not for all of the eventual Top-10 finalists. Gina Glocksen, who's from a suburb of Chicago, and Chris Richardson, who's from the middle of nowhere, Virginia, both got jaywalking tickets only minutes after getting to the hotel. Welcome to California.)

After a few hours basking in the glow of the Pacific, we went back to the hotel, and while the girls went on their field trip (to the aquarium, which freaked out one of the contestants, who was deathly afraid of fish), we dived into more auditions for the Big Three. As usual, these were sung a cappella, and I went for more Stevie; this time, I tried "Lately." I sang the entire song to Paula, staring directly into her eyes the whole time. She gave me the biggest goo-goo eyes I'd ever gotten, and I felt great about myself: I was in California, crooning one of my favorite songs for Paula Abdul.

Phil Stacey

Paula thought Sanjaya was adorable, and believe it or not, Simon was very impressed with his vocals throughout the week.

After I finished, she gave me the hugest smile and said, "Oh, Sanjaya, that was great. Terrific. You have so much potential. You're going to the next round."

And the next round was the next day. And the next day was group auditions.

As is the case with any reality television, when you're being judged in a group situation, things can get problematic, because you're forced to rely on how your teammates perform, and as the saying goes, your team is only as good as its weakest link. If I got cut because of a mistake that I made, I could deal with that, but taking the fall for somebody else's screwup, or laziness or ambivalence would be hard to live with. Making matters more difficult was that it wasn't about only how well we sang, danced, choreographed, and arranged our material, but also how well we worked together. Now, I generally get along with everybody, but who knew if everybody in my group would get along with me?

We chose our teams that night, and on paper, my crew seemed relatively solid: me, Shyamali, Jordin, and a girl who was both a choreographer and a trained opera singer, who we'll call Opera Girl. I liked our blend of skills: I was the gospelly one; Shyamali was the jazzy one, Jordin was the soulful one, and Opera Girl was the perfect-pitch one.

Opera Girl was kind of bossy and decided to take the reins, but since the other three of us were pretty chill about life in general, we rolled with it. Plus, none of us were choreographers, so we figured if somebody was going to be in charge, it may as well be her.

They assigned us Maxine Nightingale's "Right Back Where We Started From," a cute, poppy 1970s soul tune. We had to learn the song, tighten up the vocal harmonies, and solidify our dance steps. And it was *way* stressful, because we only had until the next morning to make it happen. We're talking twelve hours, which meant we'd have to pull an all-nighter, and then pray that we were one of the last groups called up to perform, so we could maybe catch a nap and avoid sleepwalking through the song.

Making matters worse was that Opera Girl wasn't the best leader in the world. Since she was a choreographer, she wanted our performance to be as much about dancing as singing. But Shyamali, Jordin, and I weren't trained dancers—remember, I'd auditioned doing only the Gospel Rock—so by the time we finished marrying the vocals and the steps, we realized that the choreography was too elaborate. So we cut the difficulty level of our steps in half. Two hours that we could've been sleeping, out the window.

Jordin Sparks

Opera Girl did go over the top, but only because she wanted it to be right. She wanted us to look good and be in sync, but she was a little intense about it, so I said, "Okay, okay, calm down, calm down." We were up until four in the morning practicing our routine, and then we had to get up at seven to perform. And we had no sleep the night before because we had to practice new songs, and it was intense. Hollywood Week was madness.

Unfortunately, we were the fourth group up. So there we were, sleep deprived and totally dehydrated, probably because the only drinking water we had access to was a shall-remain-nameless brand that, rumor has it, is spiked with salt. You see, if there's salt in the water, your thirst will never be 100 percent quenched, which means you end up buying more bottles. Even worse for us, you don't retain the fluid you need to sing and dance well on zero rest.

Our vocal arrangement was fairly straightforward and gave everybody a chance to shine. Shyamali went up and sang the first verse, then we did the chorus in unison. I had the next verse, then another unison chorus. Jordin followed suit, and then up went Opera Girl.

Now, Opera Girl was a wonderful singer—plus she had that perfect pitch, which is always impressive—and she did a lovely job on her verse, but she *waaaaaaaayyyyyyyyy* overdid her dancing. She ran across the room, did some midair twirls, and threw her hands up in the air and waved them like she just didn't care. Since she was so focused on her dancing, her singing wasn't as good as it could've been. (Why do you think Britney Spears performs with a prerecorded track in concert? So she can simultaneously dance and "sing" without losing her breath.) The three of us looked at one another sideways, and I'm sure that Shyamali and Jordin were thinking the exact same thing that I was: *She's a good singer, but nobody can hear her because she's running around the room so much. She's killing us.*

After we finished, the Big Three were quiet, seemingly stunned. Simon took a deep breath, rubbed his eyes as if he'd just woken up—ironic, considering we were the ones who hadn't slept—and drily said, "I don't think any of you can make it all the way. I don't think any of you has what it takes to win. But I'm not going to cut anybody. I'm not sure why, exactly. I'm just not."

We were the first group to make it through as a unit. But

according to Mr. Cowell, none of us were good enough to become the next American Idol. I wonder how Jordin Sparks feels about that . . .

The next day, we had another solo audition, and I think the judges were as exhausted as we were, because the comments were short and uninspiring, and mostly along the lines of "Sounds good" and "Wonderful" and "Needs work." It wasn't a particularly memorable or noteworthy audition, other than the fact that the first singer, Antonella Barba (she of the infamous Internet pictures), sang Stevie's "Until You Come Back to Me." Then the second singer up sang "Until You Come Back to Me." Then the third singer up sang "Until You Come Back to Me." Then yes, the fourth singer sang "Until You Come Back to Me." I was the fifth singer, and I sang "Some Kind of Wonderful." I don't know, maybe by the time I got up there, the Big Three were so fried on Stevie that they didn't have the energy to be constructive or cranky.

Jordin Sparks

When he did "Some Kind of Wonderful," that was the first time I heard him sing for the judges other than at the group auditions, and he killed it. I was so proud of him. I love Sanjaya's singing, and I will stand up and defend him to anybody, because he's for real. He's got such a sweet voice, and an amazing tone. He's so soothing.

Right afterward, I sat down with Cat Deeley for my first real interview. Before the cameras started rolling, she asked me some small talky stuff ("Are you having fun?" "How well do you think you're performing?") to get me comfortable, then she said, "Okay, let's start. My first question is, What have the judges said to you?"

The lack of sleep and the water-that-shouldn't-have-had-salt-in-it-but-probably-did deal caught up with me, and I went blank. "Uhhhhhhhhhhhh. Ummmmmmmmmm. Er-rrrrrrrrrrrrrrrrrr."

But then, like a voice from heaven, something came over the loudspeaker: "All contestants, please report to the stage immediately. All contestants to the stage now."

I popped up from my chair and told Cat, "Nice talking to you! Gotta run!" And I bolted.

As I sprinted away, Cat called, "We'll get you next time, Sanjaya, okay?"

I called back, "Yeah! Whatever! Can't wait!" But that was my low point in terms of interviews. After that, I kept getting better at talking with Cat, as well as with everybody else who stuck a microphone in my face. Honestly, I couldn't have gotten worse.

Phil Stacey

During Hollywood Week, we could hear ourselves singing really well because we were in small rooms, so people that sounded good then might not have sounded as good later on.

By the last day of Hollywood Week, there were sixty people left, and they had to let twenty of us go. Rather than tell us one at a time who'd be moving forward, they divided us up into three groups of twenty, put us in three separate rooms, and told us to sit against the wall in single file and not say a word. We didn't take their command of silence too seriously—we're talking about a roomful of artistic ADD types who almost always have trouble sitting around and doing absolutely nothing—so we started whispering to one another. One of the producers glared at us and yelled, *"I said no talking! Just be quiet and think about what you've learned this week!"* It was like kindergarten. Or maybe even preschool. The reason they kept shushing is that they wanted to get B-roll of us looking mopey, sitting, waiting, fretting, contemplating, and, in some cases, freaking out.

Phil Stacey

We all knew there would most likely be a younger guy who ended up in the top group. Sanjaya beat out another seventeen-year-old singer. Both of them were impressive vocalists, but Sanjaya had that thing.

They stuck Shyamali and I in separate rooms, which I'm sure was a very conscious decision, because if we were in the same room, there'd be way less drama. (I mean, even I would admit that B-roll of the two of us staring into outer space, probably thinking about what the other was going through, would make for great television.) My room was filled with people who were obviously going through: Jordin, Phil, Melinda, and a really excellent singer named Tommy Daniels. I thought,

Wow, I probably made it, because if Simon and everybody sends a group with Jordin, Phil, and Melinda home, they're really stupid. I don't know why I'm in this group . . . but I'm glad I am. I didn't know who was in Shyamali's room, but I hoped it included people like Chris, Gina, Antonella, LaKisha, Chris Sligh, Blake Lewis, and all the other performers who deserved a shot at the top prize.

Jordin Sparks

I couldn't believe how they did that room thing. We were all nervous, and high-strung, and tired, and we all just wanted them to come in and tell us so we could go to sleep, or get excited, or whatever.

Finally, after what seemed like hours, the Big Three sauntered in. Simon gave us a disdainful glare, shook his head, then smirked and said, "Congratulations. You're all going through."

It was pandemonium. Everybody was hugging, high-fiving, screaming, trash-talking, shaking the judges' hands, and having a great time . . . everybody, that is, except for me. All I could think was, *What about Shyamali? What about Shyamali?*

I ran out into the hallway and asked one of the production assistants where Shyamali's room was. She pointed to her left and said, "Down the stairs." I sprinted across the hallway, a cameraman right at my heels. The whole time, I was praying that she'd made it to the final forty. She was my security blanket. She'd gotten me through the Seattle auditions, she'd gotten me through the second round, and she'd gotten me through Hollywood Week, and I wasn't confident that I'd be able to go any further without her. Whenever I got nervous, upset, or scared, I'd think, *Okay, I've got Shyamali, and that's all I need*, and I'd feel much better.

When I made it downstairs, she was leaning against the wall, bawling her eyes out, and a cameraman got the shot they'd all undoubtedly been dreaming of since they saw us at the Key Arena: me clutching my sister, both of us crying in each other's arms because one of us had gotten cut. They knew they'd never get a sibling rivalry shot, because they quickly realized that there *wasn't* any sibling rivalry, so to them, this was probably the next best thing.

I found out later that Shyamali started crying when she saw the nineteen people who were in the waiting room with her. No Chris, no Gina, no LaKisha, no nobody. Ironically, a couple of the singers said to her, "I'm so glad you're here, because there's no way they'd cut you, so that means we're safe."

During the entire *Idol* process, I was very caught up in the moment, and didn't think about much other than what was happening right that second. I was aware that if I made it past the third or fourth cut, my life would change dramatically. But that wasn't something I dwelled on; it was way in the back of my head. My plan was to keep real and grounded, to go with the flow, to take each day and each audition one at a time, and to have as much fun as possible.

But I knew it would be way less fun without my sister around.

Walking the Green Mile

Even though it was filmed a couple of months later—January 23, 2007, to be exact—the Green Mile was an extension of Hollywood Week. And for sixteen of the forty people who made it past Hollywood Week, it was indeed execution day.

The Green Mile doesn't involve any performing. You're being graded on your cumulative performance up to that point, as well as your potential, your personality, and whether or not you'll make for good television. And then there's the small matter of your background check. Some people during my season were supertalented, but they got cut during the Mile because the myth of their lives didn't match the reality of their background.

Jordin Sparks

We got up at six a.m. to start taping at seven, and we waited. And waited. And waited. Finally the judges showed up at one o'clock in the afternoon. I told Sanjaya, "Oh, that's nice. We could've been sleeping this whole time."

They try to make it this big, dramatic deal, because they want big, dramatic television. We were sent one at a time up an elevator and let off on a barren floor. We then walked down a long hallway, which led to a big, empty room. And who was in the room? Simon, Randy, and Paula. And what were they there for? To tell us whether or not we were going home. And what was I doing on my way down the hall?

Pooping my pants.

Jordin Sparks

I had my turn with the judges before Sanjaya went up, and after they told me I made it through, I went back downstairs, and Sanjaya was the first person I hugged. He pulled me into a big bear hug and yelled, "Ohmigod!!!" When he made it through, we were both so incredibly excited that we were going together. Having somebody there that I'd bonded with was special. I couldn't wait.

Paula told me how much I'd grown. Randy asked after Shyamali. (I think he might've had a little crush on her.) And Simon told me I'd made it to the final twenty-four.

Phil Stacey

> *Sanjaya, Chris Sligh, Chris Richardson, Brandon Rogers, and Blake Lewis were pretty much the only people I'd become really friendly with, so on Green Mile day, I mostly hung out with them, and it was great to have the support, because that was a tough day.*

I ran to hug my mother, and we jumped up and down and generally celebrated like nuts.

I found out later that while I was acting the fool, my smiley-face boxers crept out of my pants, and America was treated to a shot of my underwear. Mom still points that out to me every so often, and I always tell her the same thing: "Hey, at least they were happy boxers."

But it was very appropriate. I was happy. My underwear said it all.

PART TWO

24

**TEN REASONS IN NO PARTICULAR ORDER WHY IT'S AWESOME TO MAKE IT
TO THE *AMERICAN IDOL* FINAL 24**

1. Each week, you're given three hundred dollars to
buy cool clothes for that week's performance.

2. When you Google yourself, there'll be 450,000 results instead of 450.

3. You're assigned a personal hairstylist.

4. You're assigned a personal clothing stylist.

5. You're assigned a personal vocal coach.

6. You get to meet and sing for the likes of Tony Bennett, Gwen Stefani, and Diana Ross.

7. You get to see Simon at his most sarcastic.

8. *You get to see Paula at her sweetest.*
9. *You get to see Randy at his funkiest.*
10. *Adolescent girls will bawl with excitement whenever they're within ten feet of you.*

The final twenty-four from the sixth season of *American Idol* was a great blend of talents and personalities: A. J. Tabaldo was a California dude who had a great feel for straight-up pop. Sundance Head was a big, goateed guy from Texas who was into Led Zeppelin and James Brown, and many of us agreed that he was the best singer of anybody that season; he just couldn't manage to get his backstage voice in front of the cameras. Alaina Alexander was a cute, bubbly girl with a pretty little voice and a sweet stage presence. The second youngest on the show after Jordin and me, Stephanie Edwards was sexy and soulful. Amy Krebs lived right by us in Seattle and was a totally all-American woman. Sabrina Sloan was one of the more mature contestants—and I don't mean agewise—who was into a lot of the same music as I was. Blake Lewis was a harder-edged, rockier singer who enjoyed sleeping in nearly as much as I did. What with his curly hair, cool glasses, and great sense of humor, Chris Sligh was beloved pretty much by one and all. Haley Scarnato was super-sweet and had the Christina Aguilera thing *down*, although for some reason, Simon thought of her as very cabaret. All the other people on the show—Jordin, Gina, Melinda, Phil, Chris Richardson, Brandon Rogers, Jared Cotter, Rudy Cardenas, Paul Kim, Nicholas Pedro, Nicole Tranquillo, LaKisha Jones, and Leslie Hunt—were uniformly cool, and for the most part we all got along well and were quite supportive of one another.

This supportiveness, we found out later, was one of the reasons why the ratings for our season were a little bit lower than they'd been for seasons one through five—there wasn't as much of the backstage backstabbing as there was in the past, and the viewers apparently wanted to see some bloodshed. We were close and genuinely enjoyed one another's company, in spite of the fact that it was a competition. Yes, you had to watch your back a bit, because once in a while, somebody tried to drop some nasty comments or play some subtle head games, but there was nothing too malicious. The mild negativity never spilled over into the telecasts, thus the slightly lower ratings. I guess some fans are way more interested in seeing people behave badly than listening to cool people sing cool songs. (That said, our relationships did fluctuate throughout the season. For the most part, we only had one another to talk to, and sometimes you needed to get away from this or that person, or, well, *everybody*.)

Phil became my older-friend-slash-uncle, and once in a while, he'd give me some crazy-intense life lesson, but most of the time, we'd just chill and enjoy each other's company. Phil was twenty-nine at the time, but our ages weren't an issue and we had no problem vibing. In some ways, I've matured faster than most guys my age, probably because I was raised by and around women, and it's practically a scientific fact that girls mature faster than boys. Or maybe it was just about Phil's natural chillability. If you're cool, then you're cool, and Phil's really cool. He's able to slip back into that seventeen-year-old mode and hang out with somebody like me. Then if he needs to, he can slip right back into his twenty-nine-year-old reality.

Jordin Sparks

Phil and Sanjaya got really close, and Phil was twenty-nine, and Sanjaya was seventeen. And Melinda and I got really close, and Melinda was twenty-nine, and I was seventeen. When I'm with Melinda, I don't remember her age, and I'm sure she doesn't remember mine, and I think that it was the same thing with Phil and Sanjaya. That was another example of how Sanjaya and I mirrored each other.

Jordin and I were the youngest contestants on the show—actually, she was the youngest; I have three months on her—so I had more in common with her than with most anybody else. We could sit down at lunch and talk about high school stuff: she could complain to me about her boy problems, and I could complain to her about my girl problems—just the kind of normal, stupid stuff that your average seventeen-year-old would talk about with another average seventeen-year-old. She was also a brilliant, experienced singer, so I picked her brain about technique and performance, and what it was like to be in the recording studio and on the road.

Phil Stacey

One of my highlights was after we'd made the Top 24, Sanjaya, Jordin, Gina, Brandon, Jill, and I were in a car on the way to some interviews, and out of nowhere, Sanjaya and Jordin started singing songs together. We all joined in at one point or another—depending on whether or not we knew the song—

creating four-part harmonies. In the midst of all this, Brandon and I just looked at each other and smiled. We loved the moment, and we obviously didn't realize what kind of impact Jordin and Sanjaya would have on the music industry.

When you get right down to it, the main reason we all got along so well—aside from the rampant chillability—was that we connected on an artistic level. We discussed music constantly, like we'd break down what we liked about our favorite artists, or talk about our career dreams and aspirations, and sometimes we'd randomly burst into song. There were moments in a hotel room, or on a bus, or backstage when one of us would start singing some stupid show tune, then two or three of us would join in, and next thing you know, you've got a four-part harmonized rendition of "Defying Gravity" from *Wicked.*

This is something they don't show on television, but that's fine with me. Those are the kinds of moments I like to keep for myself.

Mother and Child Reunion

There was one notable similarity between life at home in Washington and life as one of the final twenty-four on *Idol*: I was living with my mother.

We were put up at a nice hotel, and everybody was assigned a roommate, except for me and Jordin. As underage contestants, we had to travel with a guardian, and in my case it was Mom. Other than the fact that I was on the show, my day-to-day existence felt like an extension of my regular life. I wasn't as independent as I might've hoped. And when Shyamali came to visit, it felt like I hadn't even left Seattle. All that was missing was a teacher asking me why I scored so well on a test but didn't bother to turn in my homework.

Our room had a kitchenette, and one nice thing about

having Mom around was that I was guaranteed good, healthy food at least once a day, which was crucial, because while the food we were getting at the craft services table was solid—Wolfgang Puck's catering company was in charge of the cooking, and there was always good stuff to choose from—a lot of it was heavy and salty, not the best way to stay healthy and in shape for our numerous rehearsals, sound checks, interviews, and performances. Mom and I didn't have to do our own grocery shopping; all we had to do was give the production assistants a grocery list, and a few hours later, our cupboard would be nice and full. Mom was in charge of the list and made sure that I had all the protein shakes and fruit smoothies I wanted.

It felt like whenever we left the hotel room, there was a cameraman following us around capturing B-roll footage. Anybody who's ever taken part in a reality television show will tell you that you get used to having cameras shooting your every move. I didn't believe it at first, but the fact of the matter is, it's true. Initially it was kind of creepy—those lenses are huge, and they look like eyeballs, and if you look into the camera at just the right angle, you can kind of see a distorted, scary reflection of yourself—but eventually they just became part of the scenery . . . even though they were *everywhere*. The producers needed us to get used to the cameras, though, because the more we forgot they were there, the more "real" we acted, and the realer we acted, the better television they got. If the cameras were there only once in a while, we'd always be aware of them, and thus somewhat on guard.

The B-roll footage was generally spontaneous, but sometimes they'd ask us to do a conversation again so they could shoot the scene from a different angle, or have us repeat something we'd said to one of the other contestants, because it wasn't loud enough.

At the beginning of the final twenty-four process, it wasn't about the performance, but rather the showbiz. We were interviewed and interviewed and interviewed, and they grilled us and grilled us and grilled us. One of the harder bits was the questionnaire for the *Idol* website. It wasn't that the questions were difficult—actually, they were quite simple—but it was tough to answer them without sounding lame. Here's my completed questionnaire:

- **Favorite male pop artists:** Stevie Wonder, Michael Jackson
- **Favorite female pop artists:** Lauryn Hill, Susan Tedeschi
- **When did you first start to sing:** Once I stopped crying.
- **Do you have any formal singing training:** Yes.
- **What other talents do you have:** Culinary arts.
- **If you don't make it on *American Idol,* what will you do:** Use the experience to further my career.
- **What are your personal goals in life:** To become witty.
- **What album would your friends be surprised you own:** My friends don't get surprised by my musical choices.
- **Who is your American Idol:** Stevie Wonder.
- **Do you have any rituals or things you do each time before you perform:** No.
- **Most embarrassing moments:** I don't get embarrassed.
- **What has been your proudest moment in life so far:** Making it to the Top 24 on *American Idol.*
- **If you couldn't sing, which talent would you most like to have:** Singing.
- **What is your definition of American Idol:** A role model.
- **Who is your favorite judge and why:** Simon Cowell, 'cause he's brutally honest.

- **What would people be surprised to learn about you:** I can independently raise both corners of my upper lip.
- **How has this changed your life:** I'm scared that I'll never be able to walk into a supermarket without someone recognizing me.
- **Do you have any lucky charms:** I don't eat sugary cereal.
- **Who are your heroes in life:** Joseph Paul Recchi Sr. (my grandpa).
- **What's been your toughest obstacle in life:** Overcoming shyness.
- **Do you think the audition process was fair:** Yes, grueling but fair.
- **If you win, who will you thank first:** My family.

You can't sound kinda smart when the questions you're being asked are kinda simple. But americanidol.com has millions of readers, and if the people wanted to know, we were happy to oblige.

Looking the Part

As mentioned, we had a weekly three-hundred-dollar cloth-ing budget to make ourselves look beautiful for that week's show. By the time we did our shopping, we knew what song we'd be performing, so we could choose our outfits accord-ingly. Some people were meticulous about matching the clothes with the tune: Blake, for instance, went from street-looking gear to sporty casual depending on whether he was singing something by 311 or Bobby Darin. On the other hand, Chris Sligh and Melinda brought their already established styles to the table and stuck with what they knew and were comfortable with—Melinda liked her classy dresses, and Chris was into the whole slacker-chic thing—and it totally worked for them.

On *Idol*, as has almost always been the case in my life, I tended to dress for the occasion. My goal was never to be shocking, or to turn heads, but rather to play around, to switch things up. Sometimes I'd dress punky, other times I'd be preppy, and other times I'd go Goth. I have a lot of different friends who have a lot of different styles, but I'm not part of a specific movement or group—like I'm not strictly emo or straight-edge—so I don't want to be pigeonholed.

I was stoked for my first shopping spree—we never had much money when I was growing up, and while I'm not either a materialistic person or a clothing fanatic, I thought it would be nice to be able to go nuts at a store without having to worry about the price tag. Before *Idol*, clothes were just clothes to me. I liked to look good, but I spent very little time thinking about new and/or interesting outfits. I usually just grabbed whatever shirt was at the top of my shirt drawer, and whatever pair of pants was at the top of my pants drawer, and unless they clashed horribly, I went with it. I wore what was clean and what matched, and as long as I didn't look like a bum, that was fine with me.

One of the *Idol* stylists took me to the Beverly Center, a hip, huge, high-end mall in Beverly Hills. We walked by a store called Politix, and I pointed over and said, "I heard this is a good store."

"No, it's not a good store . . . it's a *great* store," the stylist said, literally shoving me toward the entrance. I didn't know where to buy cool clothes in Los Angeles, so I had to rely on the stylist's word. (Being that I had some TV cash to play around with, I grew to love the shopping in L.A., especially on a certain half-mile strip on Melrose that every Los Angeles clotheshorse is intimate with. The boutiques there are head and shoulders above what you'll find anywhere else in the country, and if you ever get on *Idol*, I'd recommend having your stylist take you there. There are also a few awesome thrift stores not too far away from Melrose, which are well worth a visit, especially if you're looking for a vintage jacket. The only downside to the thrift places is that when it comes to men's tops, the selection is limited for people who weigh more than 130 pounds. I was 125 at the time, so it was cool.)

We poked around, and right away I found a sweet shirt. I checked out the price tag: $250! I thought, *That can't happen. I can't blow practically my entire budget on one shirt.* It was disappointing, but then I realized I was in downtown Los Angeles, and I couldn't expect to pay suburban Washington state prices. If I went to Ross's in Seattle, I knew I'd come away with one cool shirt and a pocketful of cash. At Politix, we're talking one shirt and an empty wallet. On the other hand, it was *American Idol's* money, but it still kind of bummed me out.

That said, during two of the weekly sprees, I sacrificed a wider selection for a single awesome item, in the form of two leather jackets that had been marked down from seven hundred dollars. One of them was a gray leather hoodie that I fell in love with the moment I put it on. It was slick, cute, and original—I mean, who'd ever seen a leather hoodie before? Not me. I wore that thing all over the place, and a few of the other singers teased me about it being my only jacket, but I didn't care what anybody else thought, because I loved it *soooooooo* much. I'd never had the opportunity to buy a leather jacket before, and it meant a lot to me, probably far more than it did to some of the *Idol* contestants who'd come from wealthier homes.

I never wore anything on the show that I didn't want to wear. The stylists gave me suggestions, but they never pushed anything on me. I think that was because they wanted us to show the judges and the world what we envisioned our image to be. They wanted us to stay true to ourselves.

It was the same general idea with the hair. It's just hair, and there's nothing wrong with having fun with it, a philosophy that a lot of *Idol*'s older and more rural demographic didn't necessarily agree with. But since they don't live in big cities, they don't realize that it's everywhere: When you walk around the East Village in New York, you'll see people with purple hair, people with Mohawks, people with words or designs carved into the close-cropped hair by their temples, people with sideburns that are two inches long and two inches thick. Granted, you don't see too many of those cuts on prime-time network television, but trust me, they're out there. As a matter of fact, if you go to any high school in the country, I promise you that there'll be at least one formerly blond girl in the junior class who has a green-and-black-streaked Bettie Page bob.

Pre-*Idol*, I didn't spend much time or effort on my hair. The wildest thing I ever did was in eighth grade. My cut back then was a little bit shorter than it was when I was on the show—I'd guess maybe an inch or two past my ears—and during one of those annoying in-between-haircuts phases, I wasn't loving the way it looked. So on one particularly bad hair day, I hopped into the shower and chopped off the entire mess . . . or at least most of it. You see, I couldn't reach around to get to the back of my head, so I ended up leaving about half an inch of patch. I also nicked myself a few times, and Mom had to put mascara all over my scalp to cover the cuts. A few months later, most of my hair had grown back, but it wasn't as long as before, and I wondered if I'd ruined it. Fortunately, it eventually made it to a length I was happy with. If it hadn't fleshed out, I would've been okay, but it was still nice to have it around.

One morning after my do had returned to its almost natural length, I was bored with how I was looking, so I wet my hair and slathered it with a ton of gel. Then I took a towel and, starting in the back, wrapped a chunk of hair into the towel, twisted it around, then pulled it out and toward the back. It took several passes to finish my entire head. Once the gel hardened the hair, I looked like Wolverine, and I thought, *Cool, I'm going to school looking like I'm one of the X-Men*. I messed with my hair and clothing once in a while, strictly because it was fun. I wasn't looking to make any kind of grand social statement.

This was the attitude I took into the competition, and not just about my clothing and hair. It was all about having fun and doing the best I could. Remember, I'd already been cut once before, so I was playing with house money. If I made it to the Top 20, great. Top 16, even better. Top 12, 11, 10, whatever. I told the interviewers time and again that I was just happy to be there, and I meant it.

Me at 6 months of age.

Me at age 5.

Me, Shyamali, and our immediate family, circa 1994.

Shyamali and me at the Simon, Paula, and Randy audition.
We're going to Hollywood!

Backstage on tour with Phil Stacey.

Another side of Simon.

Backstage at the *Idol* finale with the great Tony Bennett.

Jordin and I hanging out backstage.

Cashing the first paycheck!

Filming a commercial in India.

Performing with Joe Perry of Aerosmith.

More fun in India.

Supporting wives of soldiers who are in Iraq.

Knocked Off My Feet

As much of a Stevie Wonder fanatic as I was, the first version of "Knocks Me Off My Feet" I ever heard was the cover by a semi-obscure R & B singer named Donnell Jones. Shyamali used to play it *constantly*, and when it came time to pick my tune to sing at the Top 24, that popped right into my head.

I should mention here that while we had a say in our song choice, the decision was not entirely ours—some of it was in the hands of the lawyers. At the beginning of every week, each of us drew up a list of tunes we'd like to perform. There wasn't a set number of songs we could pick; sometimes I'd give them three, and sometimes ten. The lawyers would then contact music publishers like BMI and ASCAP and find out whether the song's composer would grant us permission to perform the tune on the show. I'd say about 75 percent of the songs got okayed, which never made sense to me. If I were a songwriter, I'd do cartwheels if somebody from *American Idol* wanted to sing my stuff live on international television in front of zillions of viewers. If nothing else, it was a 199 percent guarantee that your record sales would go up. For instance, I bet the group Jet blew tens of thousands of dollars when they didn't let me perform "Are You Gonna Be My Girl," because even if I did a lousy job with it, lots of people would be introduced to what I believe is a great song. The only thing that I could figure is that some of these musicians had a snobby attitude toward *Idol*, kind of like my indie friends back in Seattle. Anyhow, the clearance process was sometimes smooth and sometimes lengthy, so we rarely knew what song we'd be allowed to perform until two or three days before the show. This meant we had to learn every song on our list, just in case nine out of the ten artists didn't give the lawyers a thumbs-up. As if we didn't have enough things to be stressed-out about.

The original version "Knocks Me Off My Feet" was on the album *Songs in the Key of Life*, which is probably Stevie's most complicated record. Most of the songs weren't in a standard format—there wasn't much in the way of verse/verse/chorus/verse/chorus/bridge/chorus going on. It was more along the lines of instrumental intro/chorus/verse/chorus/bridge 1/chorus/bridge 2/verse/verse/chorus. Okay, that's an exaggeration, but Stevie had some tough stuff on that album, much tougher than "Signed, Sealed, Delivered" and "Until You Come Back to Me."

Some people think "Knocks Me Off My Feet" is the hardest song on *Songs in the Key of Life* (because of all the key changes, I personally would vote for "Summer Soft," but that's just my humble opinion), and after we all found out it had cleared, Phil Stacey asked me if I thought it might make more sense to start off with something easier. I appreciated his advice but said, "I love the song, and I'm going to give it a shot. If I get cut, I get cut. At least I got some cool clothes out of it. Plus I got to meet you guys, so it's all good."

Once we'd chosen our song, we'd get together with the show's vocal coaches and/or accompanists, and we'd work out the arrangement. I'd never done any arranging before, so although I made suggestions, I left it mostly in their hands. They all had been doing it for a long time, and they wanted us to give the best performance we could give, and they were all really nice and nurturing, so I trusted them a whole lot.

I didn't have any particular concept for how I wanted to sing "Knocks Me Off My Feet," so I just took the accompanist's suggestions, most of which were pretty much along the lines of "Stay true to the spirit of the song." To me, that meant do it like Stevie. I knew that would be impossible—that first recording is so intense that even Stevie can't do it like Stevie anymore—but I'd do the best I could and, above all, have fun with it. The tune's difficulty made it harder to have fun than if I'd chosen, I don't know, "Twinkle, Twinkle, Little Star," but whatever.

Despite me not being as concerned as other people about whether or not I'd become the next American Idol, the week of February 22, 2007, was unbelievably nerve-racking. I wasn't as scared of being cut as I was nervous about screwing up. Also, I wasn't necessarily looking forward to what Simon had to say about my performance, but I shoved that into the back of my mind. If he was going to be mean to me, there was nothing I could do about it. I also took comfort in the fact that he'd probably be mean to almost everybody else.

Ryan Seacrest, on the other hand, was nice to everybody (except for Simon, that is), and he had the natural ability to put people at ease, so when he came over to interview me before I sang, I felt a bit less anxious.

He said, "Who's going to be the next Taylor Hicks? Is it going to be Sanjaya Malakar?" I thought that was really nice of him to compare me to Taylor, who's one of the most amazing *Idol* performers ever. He then asked me, "Sanjaya, we saw you were very emotional in the auditions with your sister. How's she doing?"

I said, "She's doing good."

"You think she's supporting you with all her might?" he asked.

"Of course," I said. "Family always comes first."

"We've got to get her out here," he said. "Did she help you with your song?"

"She actually brought the song to me."

"And what do you think about the song?"

At this point I was getting anxious, so I started keeping my answers as short as possible. "I love it." That was about as short as I could get.

"Is it difficult," Ryan asked, "or easy, or risky, or safe?"

"I think it shows off my voice enough to get my message across."

Ryan smiled, gestured over to the Big Three, and said, "If they give you a hard time, are you ready to go back at them? You ready to fight down there?"

He was clearly teasing me—even though we'd only spoken a handful of times, he was well aware that I wasn't the kind of guy who'd get into it with Simon Cowell—so I just said, "Yup." The audience chuckled a bit, which made me feel good. He wished me luck, and I thanked him and gave myself a quick little pep talk:

Your new blue button-down shirt is cool and your hair is in good shape, so you look okay . . . your throat feels nice and clean . . . you know Shyamali's at home watching . . . you know Mom's in the wings supporting . . . you can do this . . . you can do this . . .

I walked over to the little round stage, hoping my knees wouldn't tremble and knock me off my feet (I'm sorry, that was an awful joke, but I couldn't resist). The pianist played the four-bar intro, and off I went. Unfortunately, he counted it off a bit slower than we'd done in rehearsal—which made it considerably slower than the original recording—but I rolled with it because, well, because I had no choice.

I concentrated on connecting with both the audience and the camera, and I kind of forgot to sing to the judges as I'd done during the auditions. Unfortunately, that meant I couldn't concentrate on how I was moving, so I ended up doing a modified version of the Gospel Rock, which wasn't going to exactly blow Simon, Paula, and Randy away.

When I hit the end of the verse, specifically the second time I sang "That makes me weak and / Knocks me off my feet," some people in the front row gave me a little round of applause and a quiet little "Woo!" It was a great way to be launched into the chorus, into the "I don't want to bore you with it / Oh but I love you, I love you, I love you."

Because of time constraints, none of the contestants are allowed to sing a song all the way through, so my arrangement ended after the chorus. This was the first time I'd ever performed as a solo act before a live audience—even though I had a couple of feature songs, I was one of many in the gospel choir—and the warm, genuine applause washed over me like the Seattle rain. I thought I was pretty good, but I've always been hard on myself, so I felt like it wasn't good enough. Still, I couldn't stop smiling. I'd made it through, and people clapped, and it was one of the proudest moments of my life.

But there was a good chance the Big Three were going to kill my buzz, so I took a deep breath and steeled myself for the worst—especially since Simon was covering his mouth with his hand and kind of glaring at me.

Randy, who was wearing an odd paisley button-down shirt that was unbuttoned over a white T-shirt, sighed and groaned, "Ahhhhhh, Sanjaya, my friend. Oh. God." (I had a hunch that him groaning "God" wasn't a good sign.) "You know what's good about this? I'm trying to look at the bright side here. Because I didn't think it was very good."

Ouch. I tried my best to keep my smile. It was tough, but I did it.

Randy continued, "What's good about it is we always talk about song choice, and this is the perfect example. Stevie was one of the best singers ever in the known world, and you try and tackle a Stevie song? Dude, it wasn't even remotely close." The crowd gave Randy a little "Booooo," and in a tone that seemed legitimately bummed out, he told them, "It was really bad. I'm sorry, dog." And then he stopped and stared at his hands. I felt bad that he felt bad, and I almost said something to console him.

But before I could pipe up, Paula said, "Sweetheart, you're a sweet soul. It comes across when you sing. And there's an easiness about you, and you have a very nice voice. I wish more of your personality and more of your force came through in your performance. It seems like you're hesitant."

Paula looked supercute in her little girly-girl dress, and she was being really sweet, but it was impossible to keep my real smile on my face. But I wanted to look cool, so I gave her the Fan Smile.

Randy shook his head. "The song's too big for you, baby." I interpreted that to mean I wasn't ready to give the song its just due. And I couldn't really argue with that. Donnell Jones had been ready to give it a whirl, but I wasn't. And that was fine—I couldn't help that I was seventeen.

And then it was Simon's turn. "The irony was, the most-used line in that song is, 'I don't want to bore you with this.' And it was, without question, the most dreary performance we've had all night."

The crowd booed, and even Randy was taken aback. "Ohhhhhhhh"—he winced—"come on, Simon."

Simon threw up his hands and said, "Half the band was asleep during it. Honestly, how long did that last? A minute and a half? It felt like an hour. There was absolutely nothing that came from me." More booing from the crowd. Yay, crowd!

Randy, as would often be the case, came to my rescue . . . sort of. "It was bad, but it wasn't *that* bad."

Simon ignored him and bulled on. "You know what, San-jaya? That's what I call a waste-of-time performance. There's nothing I could take from that." Ironically, his criticism was so general that there was nothing I could take from *that*. "It was just dull."

Ryan hopped up on the stage and said, "Sanjaya, I've got to give you a chance to respond to Simon. You can't just take that."

I said, "Well, I appreciate his honesty?" I said it as a question, because I couldn't decide whether or not I actually did appreciate it.

Ryan screwed up his face and said, "You do? Why're you going to stand here and take that? Do you agree with him? Tell him he's wrong! Tell him you can do better!" A lot of people make fun of Ryan Seacrest for reasons I can't really figure out, but I think he rules.

I said, "Well, I know I can do better. I know that I can definitely put my personality out there. And I just hope that America can see that and disagree with Simon." I tried to make eye contact with Simon, but it was tough. I wasn't seeing any love there.

Simon said, "I'll tell you what. They'll like your hair."

That came out of nowhere. "Oh, thank you!" I said. Some people asked me later if I was being sarcastic. I wasn't. I'll take any compliment from Simon Cowell I can get, even if it's kind of insincere and weird. "I'm sure they'll like yours too."

After Simon thanked me, Ryan turned to the judges' table and said, "Paula, what can he do if he makes it through? What can he do next week to try and be a little bit better?"

I was eager to hear her answer, because I thought she might be able to tell me something that would actually help me improve. She shook her head, sighed, and said, "You're seventeen. He's seventeen, man. He's got to get out there and start performing."

Simon scoffed, "That has nothing to do with it."

Ryan and Randy asked in unison, "Age is not a factor?"

Paula asked me, "Sanjaya, how often do you get to go out there and perform? Truthfully."

I knew this was my biggest disadvantage in the competition. I had practically no experience, whereas people like Jordin and Phil had been touring and recording for years. "Probably not as often as the other ones."

Paula clapped her hands once. "Exactly."

Simon asked Paula, "So what're you trying to say?"

Randy jumped in. "She's saying that he doesn't have that much experience." It's weird to hear people talking about you right in front of your face.

Ryan asked me, "Do you think you're advantaged or disadvantaged by being so young? You're our youngest guy, right?"

I looked down at my new shoes. "Yeah, I'm the youngest guy. I think I can learn from other people, and I think that's an advantage. But I do have a lot less experience." *Not a bad answer*, I thought.

And then Ryan read the 1-888-vote-for-Sanjaya number, and six minutes after it had started, my first live appearance on national television was done.

Melinda Doolittle

I love the song "Knocks Me Off My Feet," and I thought he did a beautiful job, but the judges weren't feeling it, and I don't know why. Maybe they couldn't hear him well in the studio. Even after all of their negative comments, he came offstage with that Sanjaya smile, and all bouncy, and his hair was going all over the place. And he said, "I can do this. I'm going to come back again. I can do this." He had that drive. And every week he made it through, he was genuinely grateful.

Despite the bad reviews from the judges, I'd completed my mission. My plan was to sing as best I could, to listen to the judges' criticism, to absorb what could be absorbed and apply it to my songs, and to come back and do it again next week.

And after Rudy Cardenas, Amy Krebs, Nicole Tranquillo, and Paul Kim were eliminated, I knew my plan had succeeded.

At least for the time being.

Amy Krebs sang Bonnie Raitt's "I Can't Make You Love Me," and she had this beautiful dress on and her voice was so sweet—it totally made me love her. I told Amy, "That's one of my favorite Bonnie songs, and you made it ten times better than Bonnie did." I can't imagine what she could've done beyond what she did during her performance. The Big Three, however, thought that her performance as a whole was dull, and after they cut her, I realized—or rerealized, actually—that being an American idol is about so much more than singing. It's about being an entire single package, and how many viewers they think you'll draw, and marketability, and connecting with *everybody*, and it's possible that the only reason I was allowed to move forward, and Amy wasn't, was that I looked the camera in the eye. Plus, it probably didn't hurt that Simon said that thing about my hair.

At any rate, it still pisses me off that Amy got cut. She was awesome.

The day after Amy, Rudy, Nicole, and Paul were gone, one of the vocal coaches cornered me and said, "I wish I'd had a chance to work with you last week. I'd have told you that the only way to make that song work is to be lively and get hot. Listen to the way Stevie did it. He went for it. That's what you have to do. Go for it. And also, you need to sing on top of the beat. You can't lay back." Being a mellow guy, I had a tendency to lay back behind the beat and drag it, and sometimes that works—the R & B singer D'Angelo is an expert at that—but sometimes it doesn't, and I think what the coach was saying was that when you have a midtempo ballad like "Knocks Me Off My Feet," you can't drag, or else the song will be a drag.

That was great advice and I took it to heart, although it would've helped if I'd have known that earlier. I wish that's the kind of thing that Simon, Randy, and Paula would tell us during judging, but I think that the non-musicians who watch *Idol* would get bored with that sort of technical music-speak.

Some contestants were a bit down after that first week, because even though they'd made it to the final twenty, Simon had trashed them on national television, and it's hard enough being called out in the comfort of your own home, let alone on TV. But I was able to stay positive, and healthy both physically and mentally, thanks in part to Mom.

It wasn't like she held my hand and hugged me and told me it would be okay over and over again. Her way of supporting was far more productive: she made me my protein shakes, told me which vitamins to take, and kept me hydrated. Mom was wonderful.

This isn't to say there wasn't any drama. We had our fair share of "Sanjaya, wake up now," and "Sanjaya, have you finished your song list yet?" and "Sanjaya, drink your protein shake." (Mom had hesitated about me doing *Idol* back at the auditions, but once she saw how much fun I was having, she jumped right on board.) It was regular mother/son stuff, but it helped keep me real.

Jordin Sparks

Sanjaya and I both had our mothers with us, so we sometimes ran away and hid together. It was awesome that we had a piece of our family there, but it was also stressful because they'd act all parenty, and we'd say, "Ohmigod, I have so much to think about, don't ask me one more thing."

A quick word about the protein shake issue: I'm not a morning person, and the last thing I want to do first thing in the morning is eat. I need at least an hour before I'm able to comfortably put anything in my stomach. So on school days, I slept until the last possible minute, rolled out of bed, went directly into the shower, and slapped on some clothes, at which point it was time for me to leave.

Mom, being Mrs. Nutrition, wanted me to eat breakfast, so she always had a protein shake ready for me to drink on the way to school. Now, I know for a fact that you can make a delicious, healthy protein shake if you come up with the proper ratio of fruit, juice, and nutritional supplements. Mom, however, was all about the supplements and tended to get a little heavy-handed with the protein powder, while skimping on the bananas and strawberries, so oftentimes her smoothies tasted like the inside of a health food store.

As bad as eating in the morning was for me, drinking one of those things was worse. I'd tell her, "Mom, I appreciate you taking the time to make this for me, but I think I'm going to throw up if I have to drink this." She had no sympathy, so what I did was drink it *reeeeeeeeeeeeallllly* slowly, so when it was time to leave for school, I'd only had two or three sips and had successfully avoided puking.

I mention this only because this happened almost every day while I was on *American Idol*. I was pretty certain that Sundance Head, Haley Scarnato, and Brandon Rogers weren't dealing with that sort of thing.

To Step or Not to Step

As long as I can remember, I've been a huge fan of Fred Astaire. The first time I saw Astaire in the awesome musical *Easter Parade*, I practically cried. I was five years old, so I can be forgiven for bawling, but I would have wept even if I was fifteen, because his singing and dancing were both so inspirational. The fact that he could dance around the room, then sing like a madman, was awesome. I'd had a few tap dance lessons in third grade—yes, I had a few moves aside from the Gospel Rock—and I had a handful of jazz and swing steps I could muddle my way through.

I also adore Frank Sinatra, and the four-CD box set *The Reprise Collection* is one of my prized possessions. It has all the songs he's best known for, and I loved sitting in my bedroom and listening to it straight through. One of my favorite things about Sinatra is how simply he sings. You never hear him doing any kind of crazy, long-winded vocal run like, say, Céline Dion. He was about singing the song, not showing off.

I've learned that lesson well, and it'll always stay with me. Sure, I can do a crazy run, but I'll be prouder nailing a straight interpretation of the melody instead of resorting to a thirty-second "Wo-ho-ho-ho-woo-hoo-hoo-aye-aye-aye." You have to be able to sing *inside* before you can sing *outside*. Just tell the story. Let the song sell itself.

From what I saw during the *Idol* auditions and performances, you can't only be about singing loud and fast. You have to have sincere emotion. If you don't sing from your heart, the judges will notice. More important, the viewers— the people who will someday hopefully buy your records— will notice.

After the drubbing I took from the Big Three, I thought it would be a good idea to go in an entirely different direction with my material for Week Two. And what better way than tapping in to my love of jazz and swing? And what better way to demonstrate my love of jazz than performing one of my grandfather's favorite songs, "Steppin' Out with My Baby"? Irving Berlin wrote "Steppin' . . ." for *Easter Parade*, and it's since been performed by everybody from Astaire, Sinatra, and Tony Bennett to Judy Garland and Mandy Patinkin. I also thought it would be a perfect contrast to "Knocks Me Off My Feet."

My look had to reflect the song, so the stylists and I came up with the idea of straightening out my hair and pulling it back into a ponytail, and wearing a fedora over it. My outfit's simplicity—button-down long-sleeve maroon shirt tucked into a pair of gray slacks—matched the arrangement's sparseness. The outfit was part of my tribute to my grandpa, an attempt to modernize the kind of clothes that he wore when he was my age. (My initial plan was to wear an outfit that matched the song's lyrics: "There'll be smooth sailin' 'cause I'm trimmin' my sails / In my top hat and my white tie and my tails." The stylists said, "No top hat, no tie, and not tails. We don't have to take the song so literally.")

Phil Stacey

I was a little worried about some of the songs Sanjaya was picking. I thought he could be this great teen pop singer, but he went out and sang "Steppin' Out with My Baby." I said to him, "Is this really the song you want to do?" He said, "You know what? It's one of my grandfather's favorite songs, and I'm here, and I'm never going to be here again, so I want to sing it." I admired that. He wanted to do performances that mattered to the people that he loved.

A couple of other contestants tried to talk me out of doing the song, albeit in a nice way. Phil, in particular, thought I should try and wow the Big Three with something more exciting. But I wanted to stay true to myself, and right at that moment, that meant paying homage to Astaire, Sinatra, and my grandfather.

So on March 1, one mere week after my true *Idol* debut, I made my true jazz debut, and I thought I handled it pretty well. I worked the stage way more than I had in any of my other performances outside of the group audition. I played to the camera big-time. I smiled a whole lot, and I was having such a good time that it was my actual smile the viewers saw, not the Fan Smile. I hoped the judges were with me.

They weren't.

After the applause died down, Randy chuckled and said, "Sanjaya, listen, man, oh, God, you know, look, you're a nice kid, and I like you, but this was really weird for me. It was like a bad high school talent show, like you borrowed your dad's hat. It really didn't work for me, dude. This was *not* good. That was really weird to come back the second week and do that. I thought it was really weak." As was the case the previous week, the crowd booed when he hated on me. It made me feel somewhat better. But only somewhat.

Paula, who I thought looked exceptionally cute that night with her straightened hair and massive hoop earrings, said, "Well, Sanjaya, you sang on pitch—"

Randy interrupted, "That's true." I thought, *Thanks a lot, Randy, now you say something nice.*

Paula continued. "You're seventeen, right? Well, you must have an old soul. I love songs like that, from that genre. I just find it odd that at such a young age, you'd do something like that."

Simon sighed, then said, "Did you like it or not?"

"I like songs from that genre."

"But did you like *him* or not?" Simon said "*him*" with total disdain. I wasn't looking the least bit forward to his assessment.

Paula, bless her heart *again*, turned to Simon and said, "I don't like *you*."

The crowd cracked up. I piped up and said, "Good answer!" Even Simon laughed.

And then Randy pointed to Paula and said, "I'm with her

on that one." I came to learn that Randy, Paula, and even Ryan totally got off on ragging on Simon. To his credit, Simon had a thick skin and usually laughed it all off. He could dish it, but he could also take it, which you have to respect.

Paula got things back on track. "I *do* like you, Sanjaya. But I think you should pick songs that celebrate your youth." I didn't agree with her opinion, but it was a constructive, lucid thought, and I think that anybody who makes fun of Paula Abdul because of her reality show or her so-called bad behavior should be kicked in the shin.

Simon said, "So you didn't like it. Great. I agree with Randy, but I would go one step further. It was like some ghastly lunch, where after lunch, the parents ask the children to stand up and sing, and then don't particularly like what they heard." He smirked, obviously very pleased with his dig. I personally didn't feel like it was one of his better zingers, and I think based on their groans, the audience agreed. "That's how it came over, Sanjaya. It came over as very weak, a little weird, and it made absolutely no impact. In fact, halfway through the song, you were whispering. I don't get why you did that, other then it was sort of dress-up time."

Like Paula, Simon had made a legitimate point—that I'd been whispering, although his definition of whispering is my definition of singing quietly—but again, I disagreed. That was a stylistic choice.

Before Simon could insult me some more, Paula asked, "Why did you do that?"

I said, "I wanted to celebrate the great years of music, the classics. And I wanted to do it for my grandfather." The crowd understood where I was coming from, and they went nuts. In your face, Big Three.

Ryan sauntered over and, more somber than usual, asked

me, "In listening to what they had to say, what kind of feedback do you get this week?"

I didn't really have time to process what they'd told me, so I gave a generic answer: "I know I have to step it up and go with my youth."

He put his hand on my biceps and asked, "How're you feeling right now?"

I said, "I feel good, I feel good. Not as confident as I'd like to, but I feel good."

But I still wanted to run and hide.

Melinda Doolittle

Sanjaya's the kind of person who will listen to any constructive criticism and take what he can from it. But at the same time, some of the things the judges said weren't really constructive. I don't know how he was able to bounce back week after week. I sure couldn't do that. That's not my nature.

One of the problems with being the least experienced *Idol* hopeful was that unlike with most of the older competitors, my lack of stage time meant that I could never completely let myself go. A lot of these people had had dozens of gigs in dozens of tiny little clubs, and they were far more assured than I was, because they had less to worry about. Our songs were chopped down to a minute and a half, and there was so much to think about in such a short time that screwups were inevitable. It was hard to shut my brain off: *Was I getting the words right? Was I moving and dancing well? Was I in tune? Was my rhythm good? Was I singing ahead of the beat? Was I singing be-hind the beat? Was my energy popping? Was I bonding with the audience? Was I bonding with the judges? Was I bonding with the camera? Is this cool? Is this cute? Is this fun? Is this good?*

The one thing I was comfortable with was vibing with individual members of the live audience. For somebody like me—somebody who genuinely likes people—it was kind of easy. I'd look for the one person who was smiling and make eye contact and smile back. That would improve my perfor-mance, which would improve the audience's response, and that would continue until it was one big lovefest. Sometimes I also like to seek out the meanest, crankiest-looking person in the crowd and try to make them smile. If I could get them to crack a grin, I knew I was doing something right.

Anyhow, I hoped that at some point in my life—ideally within the next two months—I'd be able to be as chill on-stage as I was everywhere else in the world. The good news was that I'd have the opportunity to work on it for at least one more week, because eight people had already been cut. Yet despite again getting trashed by the Big Three, I somehow didn't. Yay!

Changing My World

John Mayer is an interesting case. His first big hit, "Your Body Is a Wonderland," is a folky love song that those indie rock snobs in Seattle would probably describe as wussy. He became a staple of soft rock radio and had developed a reputation as a musical lightweight. I don't think he liked being lumped in with the Lifehouses and the Jesse McCartneys of the world, so he went about tweaking his image. He did a guest shot on *Chappelle's Show*, and was truly hilarious. He got enough tattoos to cover a small skyscraper. And he made a handful of hard-rocking, bluesy albums that demonstrated he'd destroyed any possible traces of wussiness. These are among the many reasons why I love John Mayer. He has a confident voice, and he's a terrific songwriter, and he seems like he has a lot of fun onstage, three qualities that I'd like to have someday.

Shyamali is also a big fan, and she'd been pushing me to do Mayer's "Waiting on the World to Change" ever since I made the Top 24. "I think it's an important song," she said, "and the combination of the lyrics and you singing it on *American Idol* would mean a lot to a lot of people." After paying close attention to the song, I agreed. Getting up in front of an enormous TV audience and singing, "And when you trust your television / What you get is what you got / 'Cause when they own the information / Oh, they can bend it all they want." It's possible this was Shyamali's subversive way of getting back at the *Idol* people for cutting her, but I didn't really care about her motivation. It was a great song, and it would address all the issues the Big Three had with my previous two choices: it worked with my youth, it wasn't too "big" of a song (at least melodically and harmonically), and it gave me the opportunity to be soulful and gospelly.

Phil Stacey

I was very excited when he did the John Mayer song. It was a more suitable choice than "Steppin' Out with My Baby," and I thought he sounded great on it . . . especially during sound check. A lot of what you see on television doesn't really give an accurate depiction of what's really going on. First of all, during sound check there's nobody in the room, and it's much easier to hear yourself, so I think that everybody performed at a higher caliber than they did when the cameras came on.

And this was a crucial week, because if I survived, I'd make it to the Top 12. If you'd have told me while I was waiting in line at the Key Arena six months before that I'd someday be one week away from being one of the twelve finalists on *American Idol*, I'd have asked you if you were high.

I nailed the tune during dress rehearsal, which didn't necessarily mean I'd nail it on the live show. But I wasn't alone. The season six contestants became legendary for their mind-blowing rehearsal performances. Phil and Chris Sligh, in particular, blew the roof off the building when the seats were empty. They sounded great during the shows, but I wish the fans could've seen what they were doing in the morning.

After I finished my rehearsal, Chris Richardson wandered over and said, "That was great, Sanjaya, but don't be afraid to let it go."

I asked, "What do you mean, let it go?"

He said, "When you get to the chorus, sing a little bit higher, or do a little lick. Don't be afraid to take a risk."

Now, I'm not one to mess around with a good song, but Chris had been getting a ton of viewer votes, plus he was an awesome singer, and I knew that he knew what he was talking about. So I put his suggestion in the back of my head. I wasn't sure whether I'd take his advice on the show, but the seed had been planted.

I dressed down a bit that night: blue jeans, a T-shirt, and an unbuttoned gray jacket. Nobody said much about my outfit, but they were all abuzz about my hair. This was the first week that the stylists did something relatively radical with my 'do. They ironed it down flat and gave me a right side part. Now, I don't like irons—using them regularly will kill your hair, which I remind Shyamali about all the time. She still uses them, even though some of her hair is fried—and I generally prefer my do to be au naturel, but the stylist had been pestering me since day one to let her straighten my hair. "You have such a great head, and I can do some really cool stuff, and you should let me go for it."

Phil Stacey

Sanjaya really does have a great head of hair, and our hairstylists like to have a good time, so they came up with different ideas they wanted to try each week. Unlike most of the other contestants, he was down. He said, "I don't care, whatever, let's do it." He was having a great time.

I finally said, "Okay, fine, whatever, that's cool. There's nothing wrong with that." And then the hair floodgates opened.

Before I started singing, they had me sit on a sofa next to Ryan; I was on his left, and Sundance was on his right. Ryan asked, "Sanjaya, are you surprised to be here this week?"

I said, "Not now. But I was when I first made it."

Ryan nodded. "You looked a little shocked when I delivered the results."

"I was," I said. "I was very much shocked." I believed that my performance the week before was good enough to make it through, but there was always the chance Simon's barbs would sway the voters, so even if you felt great about the way you sang, you couldn't be certain what was going to happen next. It was in the hands of the viewers, and I did my best to avoid reading the press and the *Idol* blogs, so I had no idea what they were thinking.

Ryan smiled and asked, "Are you ready to make it into the Top Twelve?"

I said, "Oh, yeah. Definitely." And I was. I couldn't wait to sing John Mayer's awesome tune. But I'd have to wait another thirty or so seconds, because that week, we'd been asked to reveal to one of the interviewers if we had any hidden talents. There was a chance my choice would backfire on me, but I thought at least some of the voters would get a kick out of it.

Ryan said, "Let's see what Sanjaya's secret is."

The world was then treated to a get-to-know-me video clip in which I discussed my ability to hula dance; I mean, I spent a couple of years in Hawaii, and it's practically the law that you have to know how to hula. They showed me doing a couple of hula moves and then saying, "I can shake my booty Hawaiian-style." I'm not sure what kind of reaction I expected from the audience, but I thought I'd get something somewhat interesting . . . or at least somewhat *interested*. Suffice it to say they weren't all that enthusiastic. I briefly wondered how this was playing with the home viewers.

But I couldn't dwell on any of that, because I had a song to sing. I wanted to tax my brain less, so before I went on, I decided to not think about dancing. If I moved, it would be completely natural; there would be nothing preplanned, which gave me one less thing on my ever-increasing mental checklist. And it turned out that the less there was on that checklist, the more fun I had. This was undoubtedly the most enjoyable performance up until that point. The Mayer tune was considerably easier than "Knocks Me Off My Feet," and I could tell that the audience was more into it than they were with "Steppin' Out with My Baby." I ended up taking Chris's advice: during the out-chorus—while I repeated "Waitin',

waitin', waitin',"" I went for it. My run wasn't a Jordin Sparks run, and my growl wasn't a Blake Lewis growl, but it was something different for me, more energetic. I didn't hit it perfectly, but it wasn't bad.

And then, just like that, it was over. While I can't say I necessarily *liked* the song better than the previous two, I at least *felt* it more. I hoped that the judges recognized that.

Guess what. They didn't.

I will say that they were mildly tamer with their comments than they'd been for the previous two weeks, and certainly a lot more abrupt. (They seemed tired, and they tended to be less wordy when they were pooped.) After Ryan asked Randy if he felt like I did better this week than last, Randy, who legitimately seemed pained whenever he dissed me, said, "To say it was better than last week is funny. It started off with no energy. He hasn't returned to the good singer we first saw." I felt pretty good about my performance—better, in fact, than I had about the first two weeks, or even any of my auditions—so I wasn't exactly sure what he was hearing. I *knew* that I was a better singer than I was three months before. And the ironic thing is I'd improved in part because of the Big Three's criticisms. I wish I'd have mentioned that to Randy.

Paula was, as usual, a lot sweeter than anybody in the room and told me, "I don't agree completely. You have a lot of older, more experienced guys around you, but I want you to raise your game. I think the guys around you are helping you be better. Get out of your comfort zone." That last thought was something I could take to the bank. "Waiting on the World to Change" was definitely a song I was comfortable with . . . but maybe *too* comfortable. I'd have to strike a balance between a tough one like the Stevie tune and a simpler one like the Mayer tune. That wouldn't be easy, and I kind of wished I had a team of A & R people helping me out with my repertoire.

But the one A & R guy at the judges' table wasn't going to help me a bit. Simon Cowell—that kind, warmhearted A & R genius Simon Cowell—said, "It wasn't as ghastly as last week, and you are popular because you are still here. But this is a singing competition and your vocals just aren't as good as some. I'm just finding the hula-hooping, Paula-hairstyle thing all a bit weird. Maybe it's your hair that's keeping you in."

Now what was I supposed to take from that? There wasn't anything he said that could even be construed as slightly constructive. I respected Simon for his honesty and his place in the music industry, but I wanted more from him. I thought I *deserved* more. Frankly, we *all* deserved more. But as hard as the judges were being on me, I never doubted that I was a pretty good singer. I mean, if Phil, Jordin, and Melinda thought I knew what I was doing, that was enough for me.

I wasn't the only one who Simon zinged with useless insults. He told Stacey that he delivered "a third-division bar-band performance," and that Gina offered "moments of complete torture," and he called Haley "shrieky" and Chris Richardson "nasally." Viewers love this sort of stuff—actually, if I'm being completely honest, I kind of enjoy it too, at least when it's not directed at me or my friends—but if he was actually interested in helping us become better singers, once in a while he'd mix in at least a few useful comments.

Apparently, Jared, Antonella, Sabrina, and Sundance could've used some legitimate help from Simon, because they were all voted off. Somehow, despite being told that I didn't have any energy, and that I was a bit weird, I made it through to the Top 12 . . . much to Simon Cowell's chagrin, who told a reporter, "He's not going to win. I won't be back if he does."

It was probably for the best I didn't find out about that until later.

Listen, Baby

For the career-minded singer, the Top 12 is hallowed *American Idol* ground. If you make it that far, you're guaranteed a ton of press, you increase your chances of landing a record deal, and on the flyers advertising your concerts, you can always write "Former *American Idol* Finalist."

I wasn't particularly career-minded, so I think that more than anybody, I was legitimately happy to just be there. I'd realized dreams that I didn't even know I had. When I was performing with the gospel choir, or singing alone in my bedroom with my guitar, there was never a moment when I thought, *Someday I want to do this in front of the entire world. Someday I am going to do this in front of the entire world.* It wasn't a pursuit; it happened as if it was *meant* to happen.

Right place, right time, right circumstance, right collection of people. I'm not sure if I believed in destiny, but this was a convincing argument for it.

But would destiny take me all the way? Did I feel I had a shot? Honestly, I don't know. There was a chance, but the competition was so tough. Phil was amazing, and the crowds seemed to love both of the Chrises (Sligh and Richardson), and Jordin and Melinda had the kind of voices that the viewers gravitated toward. Gina, Blake, LaKisha, Haley, Stephanie, and Brandon were all damn good too, so I knew that I'd need to step it up if I wanted to make it to the Top 11, let alone the Top 2.

I thought it would be nice to revisit the R & B vibes of my youth. My house was always filled with music, but the one overriding sound was soul, especially Motown. The Four Tops, the Temptations, Smokey Robinson and the Miracles, the Jackson 5, and Gladys Knight and the Pips would blast out of the speakers, whether we were in Seattle, Hawaii, or California.

And the timing for my soul journey couldn't have been better, because our mentor for the week of March 14 was Diana Ross.

Once you hit the Top 12, each week for the rest of the season, the show welcomes a guest musician to take part in the festivities on some level. Sometimes it's part of a stylistic theme (e.g., Latin Week, Country Week, or British Invasion Week), and sometimes it's about featuring a specific artist's music, as well as music that they cite as a personal influence. (We're approaching season eight as this is being written, and I just found out Mariah Carey, Dolly Parton, and Neil Diamond are three of the guests. We had awesome guests in season six, but I sure would've loved the opportunity to sing for Mariah.)

I wasn't a huge, devoted Diana Ross fan, but I respected her as an artist, and even more so after meeting her. She's incredible at what she does—her energy and musicality are off the charts—and I was in awe. Everybody else was too.

The question for me was, *What Motown song should I do for Diana Ross?* I wanted to impress her—actually, I would've been happy just sitting across the piano from her. If I sang well for her, great, but if not, at least I could say I spent a little bit of time in her presence. Having Diana Ross mentor me would be like having van Gogh teach me how to paint.

Considering that Diana was on the show, I was certain we'd be able to have any Motown song cleared that we wanted. I considered and rejected Smokey Robinson's "Ooh Baby Baby" and the Temptations' "My Girl" in favor of "Ain't No Mountain High Enough." It was inspirational, it was soulful, and I knew that if I did it right, I could get the studio audience on my side, which meant the Big Three might be on my side, which meant a better shot at making it through to another week. Also, this was the first time we'd be performing on the big stage, and I knew that I had to come out with a big song. No more "Steppin' Out with My Baby" action.

Seeing the studio rearranged for the big performances was bizarre. The stage was huge and took up the area where the little stage used to be, as well as the green room, and the entire backstage area. You'd never guess watching on television that the Top 24 stage was in the same room as the Top 12. It was a bit intimidating. Fortunately, early in the week they gave us plenty of opportunity to practice with the new layout.

Working a big stage is a whole different game. It gives you the chance to make your performance more theatrical, something that a number of us needed to do. Melinda, for example, was one of the two strongest female singers that year (Jordin being the other one), but she had a tendency to stay planted in one place. I knew she'd go far just on the potency of her voice, but the only way she'd win was if she learned how to work the room.

Which was exactly the case with me.

I was unbelievably nervous before my session with Diana, just as nervous as I'd been throughout the entire process. I said hi and checked her out. Her hair was *huge* and she was wearing a cute black short-sleeve dress with a black wife-beater over it.

I think she could tell I was freaking out a little bit, so she tried her best to put me at ease. "What song are you going to sing, sweetie?"

" 'Ain't No Mountain High Enough.' "

She smiled. "Sounds great. Let's hear it."

I didn't have the pianist play any intro; I just launched in there with "Ain't no mountain high / Ain't no valley low." She stopped me and said, "If you're going to do it like that, you're going to have to be *point on.*" I understood exactly what she meant. She wanted me to come in strong, confident, and on the beat. No laying back. No jumping ahead. Just one-two-three-four *boom.* (Actually, it would be one-two-three-four-one *boom,* because as anybody who's listened to the song a million times knows, the first word lands on the second beat.) Her biggest concern in general was my ability to keep a steady tempo. She asked, "Do you tap your foot on the beat?" I'd never really thought about it, so I kind of shrugged and mumbled something. She said, "Well, you should." And then she reiterated something that Paula had been saying since day one: "You also need to move around, and get *into* it. Can you dance? You should! Get your soul in there! Feel it in your body!"

I said, "Oh. Thank you." After the battering I'd gotten from the Big Three, I was kind of hungry for some positivity from somebody important. And I'll always remember what she said during the postsession interview that was shown on the air:

"Sanjaya is about love. You just want to care for him. There's something in his spirit that is the winning ingredient."

Wow. That rocked. Somebody loved me. Amazing.

Then she added, "And it's not his hair, okay?"

This hair thing was getting out of control. I'd only had two "weird" hairdos, and I was befuddled as to why people kept talking about it, and how it became a phenomenon.

That week's outfit-hair combination was the mellowest since week one. My clothes were almost on the preppy side: a gray-and-white-striped V-neck sweater over a white button-down shirt, and simple gray slacks. My hair was teased up in a sort of Afro, and it looked a little bit like Chris Sligh's big old mop. As a whole, I thought it was a pretty good stylistic package. It might not have had much to do with the song—if I was thinking Motown, I might've gone with a white suit à la the Temptations, or maybe a shiny green shirt unbuttoned too low à la Marvin Gaye. But it was fan-friendly, and I really wanted to make it through the week, so I didn't want to give anybody any extra reasons to vote me off.

And then it was time to go on. Ryan, from his perch behind the Big Three, said, "This was Diana's first number one as a solo artist. Can Sanjaya own it tonight? 'Ain't No Mountain High Enough.' Here is Sanjaya Malakar!"

I started out standing on the far side of stage left and tried to amp up my energy from the get-go, starting out with a vocal run that I thought Chris Richardson would appreciate. Heading toward the chorus, I strutted in rhythm toward the center of the stage, raising my hand to the heavens above. I more or less did a modified version of the Gospel Rock that involved periodically lifting my feet off the ground. With the shortened arrangement, the key change came seemingly immediately, and that was the most difficult part of the tune, but once I got past it, I followed Diana's advice and got into it, got my soul in there, and danced. And she was right. I had a blast.

The audience had only been applauding for about three seconds when Randy burst in. "Sanjaya," he said, "what's going down, dude? What is really going down, dog? Yo, man. Wow. Dude, I don't even know what to say, man. I'm like . . ." and then he started chuckling. I had no idea where he was going with this. Was he actually about to tell me something nice? That he recognized I'd dialed up my energy level? That I'd gotten my soul out there?

None of the above. "Dude, it wasn't very good," he said. "That song was almost unlistenable for me. It was really, really weak." And this was coming from Randy. I could only imagine what Simon was going to have to say. "But you know what I love about you?" he continued. "You know what I look forward to every week? Dude, you throwin' down some different 'dos. The hair is rockin'! Dude, if this was *Hair Idol*, you'd have it jumpin' off. You know what I mean?"

I gave him a Fan Smile. What else could I do?

And then it was Paula's turn. "Sanjaya, I can understand why Diana said you're pure love, because you are. You're the sweetest soul, and when you smile, it warms people's hearts.

It really 'do. You sang on pitch. I understand what Diana was saying about starting it off so you can really grab the audience. When a song like that happens, you've just got to let go. And that's the thing we've been trying to say. You've got to explode with your vocals now. You've got to really jump out with reckless abandon and *go*. You look adorable, though."

Again, something constructive from Paula Abdul. She is pure love.

However, that night, Randy wasn't. He wouldn't let the hair thing go. Simon was about to do his thing when Randy said, "You're hair's poppin'."

Paula said, "He didn't do a bad job—"

And then Simon interrupted. "Look. When you hear a wail in Beverly Hills, that is where Diana Ross is watching this show."

The audience let out a collective groan. Paula gave me a sympathetic look, then turned to Simon and said, "*What?!*"

Simon threw his hands up in the air. "She's going to freak when she hears this. The only similarity is the hairstyle." He couldn't even look me in the eye. The crowd went from groaning to booing. At least somebody was on my side. "I don't know what else to say." And then the booing got louder. Simon checked out the audience and continued. "Sanjaya, look, I'll say something positive. Ummmmmmmm . . . how old are you?"

"Seventeen."

"Right. You're very brave. I'll give you that. You're brave."

Ryan, looking very spiffy in what had to have been an insanely expensive three-piece suit, came over and said, "The courage of Sanjaya Malakar. I think everybody wants to know what's going on inside of your head when you're listening to them give you feedback tonight."

"I . . . I . . . I . . . I don't even know. I listen to the positive things, but sometimes—no offense, Simon—but your first comment, I had no idea what you were talking about." I waved my hand in the air and said "Whoosh," as if to say it went right over my head.

Simon said, "What I meant to say was, when she listens to this on TV, she'll scream."

Melinda Doolittle

I ended up being the oldest one out there, and because of that, everybody called me "Mama." The only people I was really comfortable with calling me "Mama" were Sanjaya and Jordin, because they were young enough that it was okay. But honest to goodness, they're both like my babies. Every week that he made it through, I was so proud of him. And I know that the show has so many obstacles when it comes to getting up on that stage, it's really hard to bring it. And it kind of broke my heart when people started talking badly about him, because he has the most beautiful voice. I'm a fan. I think he's wonderful. He's all boy, though. He had moments where he tried to lick my face, or climb on me like a monkey, so that was something I had to get used to.

Ryan pointed at Simon. "He wasn't talking about the marine biology aspect of sea life. It's more about an audible sound." He put his hand on my shoulder and said, "Well, good luck. Do you feel like you should be here next week?"

Jordin Sparks

He was like a brother to me, but like a lot of brothers, he could be so annoying. One of his favorite things to do was to come up to you, then tell you he loved you, then lick your face. Now, since he was like a brother to me, I had no problem telling him to shut up, or back off. Sometimes I'd even have to smack him.

He looked like he wanted me to keep talking, to say something controversial, or maybe even to cry, but what else was I going to do? Should I have told Ryan that I should be there instead of Stephanie, or Gina, or LaKisha, or poor Brandon Rogers . . . who eventually got voted off that night after nailing "You Can't Hurry Love"?

So I just said, "Yeah." And even though I finished in the bottom two of the voting, I honestly believed it.

"Starvation for Sanjaya," Part One

On March 16, a girl who called herself "J" posted a video of herself on YouTube. She stared right into the camera and, without cracking a smile, said, "I'm here to announce that like many Americans, last week I tuned in to *American Idol* to find that Sanjaya Malakar had not been eliminated from the competition. As a result of this, I'm going on a hunger strike. I'm doing this because I believe that other more talented contestants who deserve a chance to win are being eliminated because there are other people who think that it would be funny to sabotage *American Idol* by voting for a lesser contestant. Therefore, I'm going to continue my hunger strike until either Sanjaya is voted off, or the producers rescind his spot in the Top 12, or he graciously steps down from his position. If you'd like to end this strike, this Tuesday, tune in to *American Idol* and vote for any contestant other than Sanjaya Malakar. If you'd like more info, or would like to join this hunger strike, please go to myspace.com/StarvationForSanjaya."

Great. First Simon Cowell, then Howard Stern, and now some random girl. But I stayed strong and kept striving. That was all I could do.

Riding the Pony

Two weeks later, and one week after I channeled the Kinks . . .

After the judges were nice to me during British Invasion Week (or what some people came to refer to as Crying Girl Week), my confidence soared. It wasn't that I had come out of my shell as a person—my shell had been broken in, like, fifth grade—but rather as a musician and a performer. Singing "You Really Got Me" was the moment when I was able to carry my offstage personality onstage. I wasn't scared to let my full energy flower anymore. My inhibitions were gone. I promised myself that for the rest of my life, I would never hold back anything onstage.

Even if I was sick.

I couldn't shake the cold that I'd had on and off for the last two weeks, a cold that everybody seemed to have caught from Paul Kim. Paul, who'd been cut about a month before, didn't like to wear shoes, and I think the fact that he walked around in bare feet all the time was the main reason he got laryngitis, which of course was the main reason that most of us got sick. Living in air-conditioning twenty-four hours a day—which is horrible for singers—and breathing recycled hotel air every night wasn't helping matters.

But following my mother's nutrition advice, I took all of my vitamins and drank all of my protein shakes, because I badly wanted to be healthy for that week's mentor, Gwen Stefani.

Now as cool as Diana Ross and Peter Noone were, I was especially psyched for Gwen, partly because she was closer to my generation. Not that Diana and Peter weren't awesome, but I'd been listening to Gwen since I was a kid—honestly, I loved her original group No Doubt more than I do her solo stuff, but she was still well on my radar—so having an opportunity to learn from her would mean a lot.

The producers gave us a list of songs to choose from, which included not just Gwen tunes but tunes that she said had an influence on her. I scanned it, and the only one that jumped out at me was Tears for Fears' "Mad World." And it jumped *hard*; after all, it was from the sound track of the movie *Donnie Darko*, and I was a *Donnie Darko* fanatic. Reading the list, I actually said out loud, "*Ohhhhhhhhhhhhhh! I have* to do that song!" It was also appealing because I hadn't performed a ballad at any point during the season, and especially after "You Really Got Me," I thought it would be a good idea to do something that I could actually out-and-out *sing*. But after considering it for a few more minutes, I realized that the tune is basically one melodic lick repeated over and over again, and it could potentially be kind of dull. And that was something that had been in the back of my head since Simon told me that my version of "Knocks Me Off My Feet" bored him: *Don't be dull.*

I was freaking out about my song choice until Mom's boyfriend asked me, "Have you ever heard the song 'Bathwater'?"

I said, "No. What's that?"

It was a No Doubt tune that I somehow had never heard. He played it for me, and it was really cool, with its shuffle groove and clever lyrics. I thought, *I could totally get into this.* So I crammed on the song, and I thought I'd learned it well, that is until I went into the studio to sing for Gwen. Before we went into the recording room to perform for her individually, she sat us all down and said, "It's really weird for me to be standing here in front of you. You guys are all famous. The fact that I'm giving singing lessons to Melinda Doolittle is kind of strange." I think Gwen saw herself as more of a performer than a singer, which endeared her to all of us. Personally, I think she's an awesome singer.

Then, one by one, we trooped into the studio. I went in after Melinda, and *nobody* liked to sing *anything* after Melinda, because she's a tough act to follow. But Gwen is a sweetheart and tried to put me at ease. When I told her I was going to perform "Bathwater," she blinked and said, "Really?"

I said, "Yeah. I'm just going to go out there and have fun with it, and let myself loose, and not hold back."

"That'll be great," she said skeptically, "but that's a pretty hard song. So good luck. Now let's hear it."

Within twenty seconds, I spaced out on one of the lyrics. Gwen was nice about it—she fed me the line—and I went ahead, trying to forget that I'd forgot, and stumbled my way through the rest of the tune. By the time I was done, I realized she was right: it was a hard song, fast, wordy, and full of twists and turns. But I was determined to plow through it. I had to. I didn't have any other choice.

However, with my hair, I had *plenty* of choice. And I decided to take advantage of it.

I had decided at the beginning of the competition that if I made it to the Top 10, at some point I was going to put together a Mohawk of some sort. I'd never done it before, but I had a bunch of punk-rocker friends, so I had some punk in me, and I wanted to honor that. Also, I had a hunch that Gwen Stefani Week would be the only time I'd be able to get away with it. I suspect it wouldn't have gone over well during, for instance, Country Week.

I told the hairstylist about the Mohawk idea the day before the live show, and he said, "I like it. Let me think about it for a while." The next morning, he tracked me down, gave my head a once-over, and said, "I have an idea."

Jordin Sparks

He told me about the ponyhawk, and I said, "If you want to do it, you do it. It's going to be something different, and people are going to talk about it." And I don't know if he'll agree, but I was the first person who told him that he should do it. And when I saw it, I was like, "Oh. My. Gosh." But I loved it. I thought it was going to look awesome on TV.

"Cool," I said. "What is it?" I felt comfortable in his hands; he'd made me look good for the last two months, so I figured whatever he came up with would be safe to roll with.

Phil Stacey

When he came out of the hair room with that ponyhawk, I told him, "You look like a centurion soldier." He just chuckled and said, "Look, if people want to talk about my hair, I'm going to give them something to really talk about."

"Let's make seven ponytails, and then shape it into a Mohawk."

I said, "Hmm. Yeah. *Yeah. Hell* yeah."

Melinda Doolittle

When he walked out of that room with the ponyhawk, I fell to the floor. He's so deliciously quirky that it worked for him.

It didn't take long for him to put it together, just about thirty minutes. When he was finished, I leapt out of the chair and sauntered down the hallway. People poked their heads out of their dressing rooms, and stared, gasped, gawked, and followed me like I was the pied piper; it was nuts. I got every kind of reaction imaginable: Some people said, "Oh, that's so cool!" Some people said, "What the hell is that?" One of the crew members said, "The judges are going to think you're crazy, and the viewers are going to think you're crazy, and you're going to get cut."

Shyamali Malakar

I was watching the show from my aunt's house with a bunch of my family members, and when I saw that hair, I thought, dude, what're you doing? My jaw dropped, and there was a collective gasp. But he pulled it off. He's the only person that could've done it. I was really proud of him. It took a lot of guts to do something that far out of the box. Actually, Sanjaya doesn't even have a box.

As I ducked through a doorway to avoid ruining the 'do—it went a good five inches up in the air—I said, "I don't care. If I'm going out, I'm going out my way."

Mom freaked out. She stared at me for a minute, then dragged me into the producer's office, sat me down, and told the producer, "I don't know if he should do this. It might really mess up his chances. People might think he's crazy."

The producer asked me, "What do you think?"

"I think it's cool."

He nodded and told my mother, "I'm a father, and I understand your position. But I'm also a producer, and this'll get *greeeeeeeeaaaaaaaaat* ratings if he goes on like this."

"I don't know," Mom said, "I'm not sure about this."

They went back and forth for a couple minutes, and while

Mom put up a good fight, the producer won the battle. And he made the right decision. The ratings were spectacular.

I knew that the do would probably overshadow my singing, but after the positive reaction the week before, I thought I could pick a tune that showed the judges I could really, truly sing the following week. That is, if I even made it to the following week.

While I was standing in the wings waiting to go on, Blake walked over and said, "Sanjaya, you really need to work that hair. If you're going to wear it, you can't be afraid to use it."

And then Ryan, who'd seen the do during the commercial break before my song, introduced me by saying, "Let's see what Sanjaya has for us, aside from the hair."

Despite the fact that they were clearly befuddled by the modified Mohawk, the crowd was way more responsive than they were for my Kinks performance, but I didn't know whether they were clapping for the song or the hair. I scanned the audience for Mom, and there she was, right in the fourth row center, standing up, and yelling and screaming, and obviously chilled out about the 'do, which was a huge relief. I knew that if the Big Three trashed me, I'd at least have somebody to console me afterward.

Taking Blake's advice, I made a conscious effort to move my head on the song's hits, so the hair would bop in unison with the beat, but otherwise, I focused on finding the balance between vocalizing and performing, a balance that I now understand takes years to figure out. Shyamali, who'd watched some of the shows from at home in Seattle, had told me that I'd gotten much better at looking into the camera and connecting with the home audience, so I made sure to keep that going; I know that people pay more attention if you simultaneously stare at them and sing. As was the case when I sang for Gwen, I forgot a few of the words—I had to change the lyrics to fit my gender, but still the original, non-gender-changed lyrics stuck in my head—but all in all, I think I did relatively well. It wasn't one of my better *Idol* performances—as I mentioned, I'm really hard on myself, and if I make a mistake, I take it harder than other people probably would—but the crowd seemed to enjoy it, and at the end of the day, that's what matters the most.

Without even letting the applause die down, Randy yelled out, "What's goin' down, Sanjaya, what's going down?" (He pronounced "down" as "deeeee-own.") "Sanjaya, dude, I didn't . . . I don't . . . I . . . I . . . I . . . I'm speechless every time. It's weird. You got the Dog speechless." (I didn't know that Randy thought of himself as "the Dog." You learn something new every day on *American Idol*.) "Now, the hairdo is definitely interesting. I kind of like the Mohawk look. I mean listen, at the end of the song, when you sang that one long note and did that little run . . . you can actually sing. All you have to do is put it out there, dude. That's what Paula and I were just saying to each other. Come *onnnnnnnnnnn*, man."

I heard a little squeal from the crowd. It sounded like Mom. I smiled.

Paula then said, "Sanjaya, if you had the gumption, if you had the ability to just totally go for it, then it would fit the wackiness of the faux-hawk. To watch you onstage when you don't go for it, it's kind of like . . . aw, come *onnnnnnnnnnn*. Because you can do it if you want to do it. It's like, you're already up there. Come on. You can do it." And I don't know how Paula feels about it, but I thought that was a wonderful moment between us. The way she said "You can do it" was so sympathetic and heartfelt and sweet, that to me, it was more than just random encouragement. I think she legitimately cared about me.

Simon, on the other hand, I wasn't so sure about. "Well," he told me, after giving Paula a quizzical look, "I presume there was no mirror in your dressing room tonight." *Surprise, surprise*, I thought, *he's going after the hair*.

I told him, "You're just jealous you couldn't pull it off."

He gave me a broad smile, held up his hands defensively, and said, "I couldn't. I agree." He shook his head a little bit, then continued. "Sanjaya, I don't think it matters anymore what we say, actually."

Randy jumped in, "That's why I'm speechless!"

Simon said, "You are in your own universe, and if people like you, good luck."

I cocked an eyebrow and said, "Well, thank you."

Ryan came over for his traditional postmortem. He stuck out his hand, we shook, and he said, "Sanjaya Malakar." Then he put his hands on my shoulders, gently turned me to my side, looked toward the camera, and said to the director, "Let's get a shot of the hair. It's like a ponytail. Or a ponyhawk." (Yes, Seacrest was the one who came up with "ponyhawk." Well played, Ryan!) He gingerly touched it. "There's a lot of ponytails in there."

I told him, "There're seven. For good luck."

He asked me, "At what point were you inspired?"

"I wanted to do a Mohawk because I thought it would be fun, but the stylist just put it in a bunch of ponytails."

"And out came that," Ryan said.

"And out came that," I agreed.

Staring at my hair, Ryan said, "You have seven reasons to vote for Sanjaya this week. Actually, eight if you count the hair." Apparently eight reasons was enough, because even though he nailed the Police's "Every Little Thing She Does Is Magic," Chris Sligh got voted off.

As a group, we were losing our friends one by one, and it was starting to hurt. But it was a competition, and that's what happens when you're playing a game.

"Starvation for Sanjaya," Part Two

On April 1, YouTube fans were treated to another video from you-know-who:

"Hi. This is J. It's been sixteen days since I started my hunger strike, and I regret to inform you that I went to the doctor the other day, and he advised me against continuing this hunger strike. I, for medical reasons, am going to discontinue the strike. However, I do intend to continue voting for contestants other than Sanjaya, and I hope that everyone who has supported me will continue to do the same. If you joined me in the hunger strike, I strongly encourage you not to continue this as well. It could be very bad for you. It could end very badly. We will be organizing a voting strategy for the coming weeks, so stay tuned to my MySpace page for information about that."

Seriously, if I knew this was going on during the show, I'd have personally taken J out to dinner.

The Voice

Before the first Top 24 show, we were given a long list of possible guest mentors. We didn't know who on the list was going to be on, or when they were going to be on, or if they were going to be on at all. All we were told was that some of these people would be working with us during the latter part of the season, and that we should be prepared. Everybody on the list was way cool, but one name in particular stood out:

Tony Bennett.

Fred Astaire and Frank Sinatra are my favorite jazz/swing singers, but Tony is a very close second. I wanted to get as far in the competition as I could, obviously, but I hoped that I could make it until whichever week he showed up. And I did! Yay!

As usual, there was a lot of hurrying up and waiting throughout Tony Bennett Week. For instance, we left our hotel in the morning to visit with Tony in a meeting room at his hotel, where we waited for a good three hours. And then he saw us one by one, which meant even more waiting. And we couldn't take naps, because there were cameras around. But honestly, it probably would've been difficult to sleep that day anyhow, *because I was going to meet Tony Bennett!*

I had planned to save "Steppin' Out with My Baby" for Tony, but I pulled it out during Top 24 because (a) I didn't know if or when Tony actually was coming on; and (b) I didn't know if I'd even be around if or when he did come on. So instead, I picked another awesome jazz standard, "Fly Me to the Moon," which the producers nixed, because Tony had never recorded it. (I've since found out that it was on an *MTV Unplugged* album he cut in 1994, but since everything worked out in the end, I won't complain.)

So I went with my second choice, "Cheek to Cheek," which, like "Steppin' Out with My Baby," was composed by Irving Berlin. "Cheek to Cheek" isn't an easy tune, but it's definitely one that is singable by non-singers, because it's all scales. Melodically, the lyric "And my heart beats so that I can hardly sleep" is a pattern that both vocalists and instrumentalists use as a warm-up exercise. That's part of why the tune is so memorable; it's almost sing-songy. It was another Shyamali suggestion, and since I'd grown up listening to Shyamali listen to the Ella Fitzgerald–Louis Armstrong version of it, I didn't need much convincing. Really, it was obvious. In fact, it was karmic.

When the clothing stylist heard I was going to do "Cheek to Cheek," he asked me, "What do you want to wear with that?"

Once we made the Top 10, our weekly clothing budget

went from three hundred to four hundred dollars, so I had a little more latitude in my choice. But in order to switch things up from last week, I wanted to keep it simple, so I told him, "All white. How about a white suit?" He was okay with white, but not *all* white, so I wore a black collared shirt underneath. And to keep things cool and modern, I found an awesome pair of white Puma sneakers. Hairwise, we decided that I'd go back to the ironed look I'd used when I sang the John Mayer tune, although this time, it had more of a wet look to it. It was about as far away from a ponyhawk as you could get.

My sniffles still hadn't completely disappeared, and I didn't want to get up in Tony Bennett's face and get him sick, so I was a little bit subdued when it was my turn to go into his hotel room. After we shook—and yes, I made sure I washed my hands before we shook—he said, "Great to meet you, Sanjaya. You're really good. I'm a really big fan of yours. You've got a sense of humor, and you sing really well. I really respect that you go up there, and you do your thing, and you're not fazed by what other people say or think. You dare to be different. And you know what? You're really handsome!"

I stared at him for a moment, then said, "Duh-duh-duh-duh-duh, thanks." That's pretty much all I could say: "Duh-duh-duh-duh-duh, thanks." This was Tony Bennett! And he said I was good! And unfazed! And handsome! I nearly pooped my pants. To have him know who I was, and to give me positive notes about my music was like . . . *what?!* It was crazy. I couldn't have asked for anything more incredible than that. Duh-duh-duh-duh-duh, thanks, indeed.

On our way back to the hotel from the Tony Bennett meeting, I had one of the weirder experiences of my life: the paparazzi started following us. It was just like in the movies: a bunch of shady-looking guys running after us on foot, or chasing after us on motor scooters, snapping photos the entire way. Yes, we were on television each week, but I still couldn't wrap my mind around the fact that people cared about seeing a shot of me climbing into a van . . . let alone that they knew who I was in the first place.

Come show night, all the extraneous stuff was forgotten: the paparazzi, the sniffles, and the lack of sleep all went out the window. It was simply about the performance. I had to stay focused, so when the bandleader counted in the band—and this week, since we were doing jazzier material, the band was full of trumpets, trombones, and saxophones—I could come in strong and on time, just like Diana Ross had told me to do.

I tried to get all lounge lizardy for this performance, tried to look suave and debonair. I'm not sure if I pulled it off, though—I was seventeen, and how suave and debonair can a seventeen-year-old look?—but I think I came across as somewhat swingin'. For the first part of the tune, I played almost exclusively to the camera, because not only was that the best way to hook the voters, but it was fun. Not to sound corny, but I'd begun to view the camera as my friend.

As I hit the bridge ("Dance with me / I want my arm about you / The charm about you / Will carry me through"), I bopped over to the judges' table and offered the fair Ms. Abdul my hand. I had no idea if she'd actually get up and dance with me, because there wasn't as much spontaneity on *American Idol* as there looks to be on television. But sure enough, Paula stood up and swayed and twirled with me for a couple of lines. I knew it was a good idea when Randy enthusiastically did sort of a raise-the-roof thing with his hands, and Simon didn't look 100 percent annoyed.

Then, just like that, it was done. Most of the arrangements

were one minute and thirty seconds long, but this one felt like it was over in a blink. I hoped that wherever he was watching from, Tony Bennett liked it.

And it wouldn't hurt if the Big Three liked it too.

Randy, who you can't help but smile with, as he has one of the most infectious grins on the planet, said, "Yo, Sanjaya, check it out: I can't even comment on the vocals anymore, but what I like about you now is you've turned into a great entertainer. You've got the different hairdos every week, you're dancing with Paula." He turned to Paula. "He's an *entertainer*, Paula. Look at him. He's ready!"

Paula giggled. "He *is* an entertainer. I get why people love you. I get it. You're charming. The vocals were a little off at the beginning, but I understand what Tony says. You've got this charm about you, and I love the suit, and the whole *Dancing with the Stars* thing. Thank you for the dance."

Phil Stacey

When the Top 10 came around, we didn't have any monitors. Chris Sligh and I were the only ones who ever used in-ear monitors during the show, and that was only because the producers had us start our songs in the audience, where it would've been impossible to hear ourselves. There were monitors under the stage, but those were for the musicians, and they couldn't put any vocals in there, because if they did, it would scream and squeal with feedback, which would've been terrible for television. It was harder for Sanjaya, because everybody else had been performing live for years, and he'd never had experience with bad sound systems. It was a big disadvantage for him, very difficult.

I was speechless. All I could do was grin, despite the fact that she'd called me out on a legitimate vocal error. The crowd, thankfully, cheered for a few seconds, so I didn't even *have* to say anything.

Simon looked around the studio for a bit, then said, "Uh-hhhhhhh, let's try a different tactic this week."

Randy rolled his eyes. "What're you going to say?"

"Incredible," Simon said. "That's it. Just, 'Incredible.' "

I never found out whether he was kidding—considering the silly expression on his face, he probably was—but it still felt amazing. "Thank you, Simon," I yelled. "Welcome to the universe of Sanjaya!"

And then Ryan, who definitely *was* joking, said, "You do a great job at staying under the radar, Sanjaya."

Gina was voted off that night. Our numbers were dwindling. We knew it was coming, but that didn't make it any less difficult.

MTV.com, on the other hand, was making things more difficult:

10 Reasons (Besides Howard Stern) Why Sanjaya's Still on *Idol*

There's one every year: An *American Idol* contestant who dominates the show despite not really having a chance at the top prize.

Some, like William Hung, don't even get past the auditions. But when they do, they shake things up every week, exasperating fans and other contestants, spawning endless chatter about their perplexing ability to avoid the ax.

This year, it's the vocally suspect Sanjaya Malakar, who has turned into a media sensation mostly because of the vast media chatter—including ours, admittedly—about his suspect vocals. . . .

So instead of trying to think of more reasons why Sanjaya *should* be booted, we present 10 reasons (besides Howard Stern) why he's gotten this far:

1: **Every Season Has One:** From Ryan Starr and Nikki McKibbin during season one to Julia DeMato (season two), John Stevens (season three), Mikalah Gordon (season four) and Kevin "Chicken Little" Covais (season five), it seems like every year, one marginally talented singer manages to make it to the finals. Personality counts—but it only gets you so far, and if elimination history is any indication, it'll probably only buy Sanjaya a few more weeks at best.

2: **The Little Girls (and Grandmas) Understand:** As we saw in week two of the finals with Ashley Ferl (a.k.a. the "Crying Girl" . . .), Sanjaya has the breathless-tween-girl vote all wrapped up, which is a huge voting block for any *Idol*. Combine that with pinchable cheeks, and you have the grandma and soccer-mom votes sewn up, too.

3: **Stumbles by Other Contestants:** Chris Sligh couldn't find the beat and Gina Glocksen said it best: "You can't rock out Tony Bennett." . . . On the other hand, while his vocals are not stellar, Sanjaya always surprises, which brings us to #4 . . .

4: **He's Got Style:** He may not be the best singer, but between the pony-hawk hairdo and last week's cheeky dance with Paula, Sanjaya puts on an entertaining show while most of the other contestants primarily stand—or sit—around.

5: **The Media Circus:** The media has hyped the question of Sanjaya's talent (or lack thereof) so much that it's only brought him more attention and, apparently, more fans. Even judge Simon Cowell has thrown up his hands and uncharacteristically admitted that it doesn't matter what he says anymore. . . . *Idol* Executive Producer Ken Warwick has basically agreed, quipping, "He's still [on the show]. One of the key things is to keep people interested—and he's certainly doing that."

6: Burnout: After six seasons, it's possible that viewers are simply tired of watching the same predictable Whitney and Mariah-esque R&B throwdowns every Tuesday night. Maybe they see Sanjaya's wackiness as a welcome shot of life into an hour of, at times, numbingly similar performances.

7: The World Loves a Trainwreck: The only thing Americans like more than peeking into the lives of the fabulously wealthy and famous is ogling their car crashes and public flame-outs (see Britney, Paris, Antonella Barba, Mel Gibson). Sanjaya's efforts to make lemonade out of lemons add a refreshing twist.

8: Pity, or Contrariness: Given the beating he's taken in the press and from the judges, maybe people are voting for Sanjaya as a way to get back at Simon—or just out of pure sympathy for the battered underdog with the 1,000-watt smile.

9: The Coattail Effect: From the hunger-strike girl to the "Eating for Sanjaya" guy who vowed to keep stuffing his face until Sanjaya's kicked off the show, from the morning talk shows to his sister (rejected *Idol* contestant Shyamali), Sanjaya is creating a whole economy of hangers-on. Kentucky Fried Chicken even got in on the action, offering Sanjaya a free lifetime supply of its chicken bowls if he rocks a bowl haircut on the show. And as any rock band knows, merchandise counts for a lot: At press time, in addition to Sanjaya T-shirts, mousepads, trinket boxes, tote bags and earrings, someone had even posted a (seemingly fake) item on eBay offering the www.fanjayah.com domain name for the low, low price of $2 million.

10: Sanjaya Figured It Out: Like William Hung, Sanjaya seems to understand his place in the world of pop culture, and after looking like a deer in the headlights early on, he's begun to embrace his renegade popularity. Presumably resigned to his minimal chances of winning, he's having fun, seeing where it all can take him, and not worrying about what the haters say—which is the best revenge. Plus, after that pony-hawk, he knows people can't wait to see what he'll do next.

Truth be told, regarding number 10 on the list, I had most definitely *not* figured it out. Truth be told, *American Idol* is impossible to figure out. Think about it: if somebody could figure out how to pick the right song, and the right outfit, and the right attitude for three months straight, they'd deserve to win.

Melinda Doolittle

When you get on a show like Idol, *and you find out what the pressure is really like, it can be kind of disheartening and hard to get through. When I would read something negative about myself, my feelings would be so hurt, and people were saying the worst things about Sanjaya, and he always bounced back. It didn't faze him. He always had a smile on his face, so there I was, twenty-nine years old, learning about life from a seventeen-year-old.*

Kiss Me Many Times

Ever since 2002, when she went from being an actress to an actress-slash-singer, I'd been a Jennifer Lopez fan. When I found out she would be our mentor for the week of the April 11 show, which was Latin Week, my curiosity about one specific issue kept eating at me: *Is her butt really as amazing as everybody says it is?* It wasn't the most mature thing to consider in the midst of an increasingly tense competition, but people had been talking about J.Lo's tush for years, and I couldn't help but wonder.

I was a little concerned about Latin Week. I didn't have a deep knowledge of Latin music of any sort—salsa, meringue, samba, and so on—but I do have a good feel for international rhythms, so I figured I'd be more or less okay. I did have one general idea, though: *I'm going to do a song in Spanish this week, and it's going to be a ballad, a song that I can sit down and flat-out sing, no distractions, no jumping up into the air, no running into the audience, no six-inch-high hairdos.* It was going to be about the music, a concept that, as I've mentioned, some *Idol* contestants have a tendency to forget or ignore.

Choosing a tune was proving to be difficult. One of the songs on my list was "Cariño," a tune that Jennifer had recorded back in 2001. It's a perfectly good song, and I'm sure I would've had a great time with it, but it wasn't the right kind of ballad. "Sway," a Dean Martin song, was also on my list, but Melinda chose that one, and frankly I'm glad she did, because it worked out better for both of us.

I was still on the fence about my song when I went into my private rehearsal session with the piano player. I followed Blake Lewis, who'd sung a Marc Anthony tune for J.Lo, and, considering Marc was her husband, I thought that was a pretty slick move on Blake's part, a genius way to curry favor with the mentor.

After I took Blake's place by the piano, I noticed a pile of sheet music, and right under the words and chord changes for the Anthony song sat a chart for a tune called "Bésame Mucho." I knew enough Spanish to translate the title: *Kiss me a lot.* I thought, *Hmm. Never heard of this one. Interesting. Maybe it's a ballad, and that would be cool.* I asked the piano player, "What's this?"

"It's something that Blake was going to sing, but he decided not to."

"Can I listen to it?" I asked. So she busted out her portable CD player and put on Diana Krall's version. Even though Diana didn't perform it exactly the way I'd expected—she did it all laid back and loungy, and I thought it would be a bit sadder—I immediately saw how I could make it work for me. The piano player kind of made a face after the song was over. "What's wrong?" I asked.

"That's a beautiful song," she said, "but I've never enjoyed it, no matter how well it's performed." I knew exactly what she meant. There're plenty of songs out there that I recognize are great but I just don't care for.

"Well," I said, "I'll give it a shot and see how it goes. If it works, it works. If not, at least I tried."

I picked up the lyrics sheet, and the pianist counted me off and I sang the tune . . . sort of. It was the first time I'd seen the words, so it was more of a half-singing, half-talking kind of thing. But it was so beautiful that when I hit the chorus, I got a little emotional. The melody was lovely, and even though I had no idea what the lyrics meant, I was touched.

We finished up and the vocal coach said, "Wow. I could tell you had no idea what you were saying, but that's the first time I've ever really enjoyed that song. Congratulations."

I said, "*What?!* Are you serious? Yay! You like how I did a song that you don't even like!" It was a sign. How could I not choose "Bésame Mucho"?

The more I thought about it, the more I wanted to sing the whole tune in Spanish, but the producers asked that I do half Spanish and half English, because they wanted all the viewers to understand at least some of what I was saying. Before I performed it in front of J.Lo—or in front of anybody, for that matter—I wanted to find out the translation of the words. I could've learned to sing it without knowing the exact significance, but then the song wouldn't have meant anything to me, which means it wouldn't have meant anything to *anybody*. It forced me to really think about what I was singing and the emotion behind it.

We looked up as many versions of the song as possible, and stumbled onto Nat "King" Cole's. He sang it in English, and made the lyrics sound sweet and cheery. It was a beautiful performance, but kind of incongruous, because the song is about a man who's afraid he'll never be able to kiss the love of his life after tonight. It's a song of desperation. The man is telling the woman, "I need to feel you. I need to connect with you. I need this kiss." Once I understood what the composer, Consuelo Velázquez, was trying to get across, it changed my entire attitude. Once I absorbed the tune's sense of desperation, I realized I had to reach beyond that, to get *inside* the song. Now that I *understood* the story, I'd be able to *tell* the story, no bells or whistles necessary.

After I decided on my tempo, and after I knew the words backward and forward, I went down to the garage in our hotel to practice a cappella. (Once we'd moved into a new hotel before Top 12 Week, I discovered that the garage was the best place to rehearse. Yes, it was dirty and dusty, and yes, it smelled like exhaust fumes, and yes, cars would sometimes come by and drown out what I was singing. But it had the best acoustics of anyplace I had access to, plus I could go down there at all hours—I didn't like to sing a song for anybody before I ironed out all the kinks. Taking all that into account, the garage made the most sense.) Three hours later, I felt that "Bésame Mucho" was ready to be heard by the outside world.

The next day, we went to meet Jennifer, and she was lovely. I dressed up a bit more than usual, not because I wanted to impress J.Lo, but rather because I'd started to understand the whole look-good-for-the-camera-at-all-times deal. Even if the outfit I wore for Jennifer was on television for only five seconds, it might make a difference. If a hundred viewers thought *Hmm, that's a cool shirt* and voted for me, that could mean the difference between staying and going. That's show business. I was learning.

We went to her hotel, and unlike most of the other mentors, Jennifer wanted to address us as a group. "Let's all cop a squat on the ground and talk," she said.

We all thought that was pretty cool, so we sat down on the floor, and as she was about to join us, one of the producers ran over and said, "*No! Jennifer Lopez cannot be on the floor! Get her a seat!*"

A production assistant ran over with a chair, and when Jennifer sat down, she gazed at all of us copping our squats and said, "This is awkward. I don't want to be sitting above you. I feel like I'm a grade school teacher and it's story time. I feel like I should have a Harry Potter book or something." Just from that little exchange, I could tell she was really down to earth, definitely one of our cooler mentors.

Then, for the next twenty or so minutes, Jennifer broke down the importance of not just learning a song's words but *knowing* the song's words. (I thought, *Wow, talk about good timing.*) "Listen to the lyrics," she said. "Learn the lyrics. Understand the lyrics. *Emote* the lyrics. Emoting is one of the most important things about Spanish and Latin music. It's where the feeling comes from." She told us that if we do it right, emote-singing could bring us to a new place without ever having to leave our homes. Then she explained that we need to know exactly what lyric comes next in the song, because if we don't know what's coming up, we won't know where to go. We took all of that to heart—first, because it was great advice, and second, she's an actress, so she knows all about emoting.

I totally understood what she was saying. It was easier to

emote with a song like "Bésame Mucho" than it had been for, say, "Steppin' Out with My Baby," simply because the song had more innate, intense emotion. I had to put myself in a headspace to sing to a woman who I might never see again, which is more intense than a ditty about taking your eye-candy girlfriend out for a night on the town.

Halfway through my performance for J.Lo, she smiled and said, "Ooh, I like Sanjaya. No, I *looooooove* Sanjaya." And then she giggled. *I made J.Lo giggle!* She told me that I should take my time with the song, that I shouldn't rush through it, that it was a really good choice for me, and that Simon would be impressed.

I thought, *Simon? Impressed? If you say so.* But maybe she was right. Maybe this was the week that would get me through the rest of the season.

That being the case, I had to be smart about my outfit. I'm not sure how smart it was to wear a T-shirt with images of a naked woman on it, but it was an abstract drawing, and you couldn't tell what it was unless you already knew. To the un-trained eye, it simply looked like a cool shirt. I also wore a sport coat, blue jeans, and Converse All Stars. As with last week with the suit and the Pumas, I wanted to look grown-up and young at the same time.

The hairstylist tried to do a finger wave, kind of a Cary Grant, old-timey looking do, so they loaded my hair with an oil-based gel and wedged it into place, and stuck me under the heat lamp for about forty-five minutes. My earrings got red-hot, and it felt like my brain cells were literally getting fried, and I was *soooooo* miserable. Finally they let me go, and the second I stood up, the whole finger wave collapsed. They immediately abandoned the concept—time was getting tight—and I thought, *Great, after I spent forty-five minutes sit-*

ting two feet from the sun, they're not even going with their plan. We ended up doing some small, shiny little curls, which I liked more than the finger wave, because I thought it brought out my Italian side.

I hadn't shaved in a few days; I was trying to grow in a beard and mustache, but I was only seventeen, so it wasn't coming in quickly at all. So the stylist grabbed a razor and cleaned up my cheeks and sideburns, then took some mascara and filled in the empty spots in my goatee. At least ten people backstage told me I looked like a totally different person, like a Latino. I said, "Not Latino. Italian."

I was stoked to get onstage, because this was what I'd been waiting for, a chance to sing a ballad. Ballads are my roots. Crooning is in my blood. I can sit down in front of a girl, sing her a slow love song, and I know that at the very least, she'll be smiling by the time the tune is completed. I couldn't wait to do that for a zillion people.

As J.Lo suggested we do, I tried to emote. And following the advice Tyra Banks gives all the contestants on *America's Next Top Model*, I tried to model for the cameras with my eyes. I practically sang the entire song to the cameras. This tune wasn't for the Big Three, or the studio audience. My *Idol* life was hanging on a thread, and I wanted this one to be for the voters . . . especially the Spanish-speaking ones.

Phil Stacey

He started coming into his own as a performer . . . even without monitors. You see things like "Bésame Mucho," where he came out and nailed it, just did a great job.

The applause wasn't loud and crazy, but rather warm and polite, but that was cool, because I wasn't expecting any yelling and screaming; it's rare to hear an audience yell and scream after a mellow ballad. Before the clapping died down, Randy said, "Yo, come on out, man, come on out. So Sanjaya, check it out, baby, check it out, you know what, you're one of the smartest contestants I've ever met, dude. That was actually really good! It was!" It was a bummer that the judges always sounded so surprised when they told me I'd performed well.

Paula, who seemed a bit more subdued than usual, said, "Yeah, it was on pitch, it was smooth, and it was nice. It was very, very, very, very nice." And that was it. I couldn't decide whether her lack of specific advice was a good thing or a bad thing.

And then, it was time for You Know Who. "Right," Simon said, "I couldn't understand a word of it, you sang like a fourteen-year-old, and I'm going to hate myself for this, but it wasn't horrible." I was so shocked, I couldn't even come up with a snappy comeback.

Jordin Sparks

The judges were always harsh on Sanjaya, but when he kept staying around week after week, more and more people tuned in to see what they were going to say about him. And I think that a lot of the viewers based their opinions on Simon's opinions. Simon certainly didn't have to be so mean, though.

Ryan came over, a smile glued onto his face, pointed at Simon, and said, "Do you realize how painful that was for him to say?"

And then he pointed at me, looked at the judges' table, and joked, "He was clearly unaware of the camera, right?"

Simon chuckled. "He didn't know it was there."

Oh, but I did. Being aware of the camera was a little trick I learned from a little show called *American Idol*. You might've heard of it.

Had I had the option to sing "Bésame Mucho" earlier in the competition, I probably would have done it, but it definitely wouldn't have gone as well. The Big Three may not have agreed with me, but I felt that since January, I'd really grown not just as a performer, and not just as a singer, but as an artist. The old Sanjaya probably would've gone the Nat "King" Cole route and happily swung the tune. But the last three months had changed me, and I performed it *right*.

Melinda Doolittle

I loved to hear him sing those ballads that were gorgeous and pretty, and our season didn't really allow for that. When he got to sing "Bésame Mucho," everybody was like, Oh my gosh, he's got a beautiful voice. He never got a chance to showcase what he's amazing at. I don't think the producers thought that out. And he sang the snot out of it. That was the Sanjaya that I got to hear backstage all the time.

However, performing something *right* on *American Idol* doesn't guarantee that you'll live to fight another week. Even if you work the room, and the camera, and the audience perfectly, and even if the judges say nice things about you across the board, and even if you're vocally at the top of your game, the viewers might decide that they didn't like your outfit, or the way you interacted with Ryan, or even something as seemingly inconsequential as the way you breathed.

I thought that Haley did "Turn the Beat Around" *right*.

The viewers didn't.

Haley was voted off.

But I lived to fight another week.

(P.S. Later that week, I heard an interview with Marc Anthony and Jennifer Lopez. Marc was asked what it was like meeting me, and he said, "I like Sanjaya. I'd like to adopt him and mentor him." When asked about what my mother would think, Marc said, "She can come too. We have room." Since I thought this was a good idea, any lustful images of J.Lo's butt went straight out the window.)

At Least I Gave Them Something to Talk About

With some reality shows, the contestants are completely sequestered and aren't allowed access to friends, family, cell phones, television, radio, Internet, books, or magazines. These shows want their people to be totally immersed in the task at hand; plus, if they speak with their peeps in the outside world, they might find out what they're doing right or wrong in the competition, and that would give them an unfair advantage.

With *American Idol*, from the Top 24 on, you know exactly where you stand with the general public, plus you're getting feedback from the judges, so it doesn't really matter if you know what the bloggers are saying. So we all had cell phones and Internet access, and we knew the deal. I kept trying to avoid the chatter, because no matter what the media or the public said about me, I wasn't going to change. I was going to stick with what had gotten me to the Top 7: hard work, choosing good songs, and having fun.

All that said, the producers strongly advised us against reading the blogs. They were afraid we'd see something really horrible about ourselves, and that that would affect our performances. They were also concerned that we ourselves would start to blog, or get into an embarrassing e-discussion with the fans . . . which is exactly what happened with one of the season six contestants.

This person—who shall remain nameless—did exactly what the *Idol* people feared: he talked smack about other contestants on their fan sites; he bigged himself up under false names all over the web; and he divulged secrets about the show on his own blog. What he wrote wasn't horrible, and it didn't ultimately have any effect on the final outcome (we think), but it was still kind of slimy. Yes, *American Idol* is a competition, but, well, *come on.* Months later, this nameless person apologized to all of us, and was so sincere about it that we forgave—but we didn't forget.

Me, I didn't go onto the blogs, so I only had the slightest knowledge of the Sanjaya backlash. My thinking was, *I can read about all this later. Right now, I'm having fun, and I'm going to keep enjoying it.* Why allow any negativity to creep in?

Even though I was largely ignorant of what the public was saying about me—and when you get right down to it, it doesn't matter what the judges say, because the voters have the final say—the day after "Bésame Mucho," I had a weird premonition:

This was going to be my last week.

Yes, I'd just delivered what everybody seemed to agree was my best performance to date, and I was on a high, but it was an apprehensive high, because this week was Country Week. Now, I've listened to my fair share of country music, and there are a handful of country artists who I enjoy, but I've never claimed to be a country singer, nor am I much of a country fan. I appreciate it for what it is, and I realize that there're a lot of really talented country artists, but it's not my thing.

I'd actually been making song choice preparations for Country Week since Gwen Stefani Week, submitting tune after tune to the legal department for clearance. I had to make sure that if I found a country song I could be comfortable with, nobody else would snatch it up. "Little by Little" by Susan Tedeschi was one of the tunes I was actually hyped about. It wasn't pure country—Susan's a blues singer, but some of her material has a country-ish twist—and I loved the song, so I knew I'd be able to get a handle on it. Unfortunately, one of the producers told me, "She's too bluesy. She's not country enough. You can't use any of her stuff."

Ouch.

I had come up with another plan. One night during Tony Bennett Week, while tossing and turning in my hotel room, I remembered that the previous summer, I'd gone up to Oregon to help my mother's cousin's new husband level out a wall that had been built on some very uneven ground. (It was hell, but it was also my first paycheck.) His daughter, who's just a couple months older than me, is both a country singer and a country fan, and she played me a tune called "Boondocks" by a band called Little Big Town. It's a neat song with some interesting lyrics ("I feel no shame / I'm proud of where I came from / I was born and raised in the boondocks"), and I thought I could make it sound good.

I pitched the idea to Shyamali, and she flipped . . . but not in a good way. "Do you really want to sing about how you were born and raised in the boondocks, and how all you want is a tin roof, a front porch, and a gravel road? Come *on*. Think about whether or not it applies to your life."

I saw her point. "Boondocks" was out. Next choice: "Pickin' Wildflowers" by Keith Anderson.

"Pickin' Wildflowers" was a straight-up, simple country

song about meeting your girl out by the woods, drinking beer, and picking wildflowers, which is a lousy euphemism for love-making. Everybody agreed that it wasn't an appropriate *Idol* song. Had Gina Glocksen, our resident Tenacious D fan, who appreciates a song with that sort of sentiment, still been around, she might've tried to talk me into it. But she wasn't, so now "Pickin' Wildflowers" was out.

My next choice was "Mercedes Benz" by Janis Joplin. Even though Janis isn't a country singer, "Mercedes Benz" was a country song, so I thought there was a chance it would get the thumbs-up from the producers. My fingers were crossed, because I had a great idea for a fun arrangement: it would start out with just me and a spoons player, then at the chorus, a guy playing the washtub would join us, after which the whole band would jump in. It would've shown a completely different side of me (granted, it was a side that didn't actually exist), and I thought it would be theatrical enough to get me through to the Top 6.

I didn't hear anything about it for a while, so I thought it would be a wise idea to have a second song prepared. I was a huge Bonnie Raitt fan—like Susan Tedeschi, Bonnie was more blues than country, something I could totally get with—and I knew "Something to Talk About" up and down, so I made it my backup to Janis, hoping and praying that I wouldn't have to pull it out. I kept working on Janis, all but ignoring Bonnie.

A day and a half before the telecast—that's a day and a half before I was going to sing for the entire world, not to mention the Big Three—I was on the main stage, zipping through "Mercedes Benz," having a good old time, when a producer ran over, stopped the band, and said, "We can't do this song, guys."

I asked, "Why?"

"Ford is one of our sponsors. We can't have you singing about Benzes."

"*Wwwwwwwwwwwwhhhhhhhhhaaaaaaaaaaat?!!* You couldn't have told me that a week ago?! Or even when I first submitted it? You waited until *now*? *Nobody* thought about this? Are you *kidding*?" It was the first time during the entire *American Idol* process that I got really upset about anything. All the hurrying up and waiting, all the lousy food, and all the harsh judging barely fazed me. This, however, was an entirely different story. I was fazed. Big-time. But on the bright side, I was comfortable with the Bonnie Raitt tune, so performing it wouldn't be much of a problem. I was, however, uncomfortable with the rest of the situation. I was already feeling weird that week, and this just made the whole thing seem weirder.

The weirdness oozed over into show night. During rehearsal, and during makeup and hair, I didn't have much to say. All I could think was, *This is the last time I'm going to sit in this hair chair . . . This is the last time I'm going to have this beautiful woman do my makeup . . . This is the last time I'm going to see all the cool camerapeople, and PAs, and tech crew . . . This is the last time I'm going to sing on this amazing stage.* It must've all been right there on my face, because a number of people came over and asked if something was wrong. I told everybody, "No, I'm chill, everything's fine." What was the point of complaining or moping? It wouldn't change anything. So I went off into the dressing room by myself and tried to clear my head. An hour later, it was time.

Before I sang, they stuck me on a stool next to Ryan, who asked me a viewer question: "If you could make one of the judges sing a song, which judge would you pick, and what song would that be?"

Being that I was psychically certain that I was down to my

last few minutes on *American Idol*, I figured I'd take one last silly swing at the head judge: "I'd have Simon Cowell sing 'Shiny Happy People,' so he could show his true personality." One of the things that I like about Simon—and despite everything that happened, despite everything he said, I *do* like Simon—is that he has a sense of humor about himself. When Randy or Paula tease him, he generally laughs, which is exactly what he did with me. He didn't say anything, but a laugh was good enough for me.

Ryan grinned and said, "That would make my day."

I nodded. "Mine too."

"Are you ready for tonight?"

I thought, *No*. But I said, "Yes."

On the surface, my performance was fine. I strutted around the stage, went to dance with the background singers, and stared down the camera—although not as much as I did during "Bésame Mucho"—and went out into the audience, the whole time wearing what I hoped was a nice smile. Now I look back and see a scared, uncomfortable young man trying to get past a road bump while putting up a good front. At the end of the tune, remembering what our mentor for the week, Martina McBride, had told me, I projected the hell out of the song's last word: *"Loooooooooooooooooooooooovvvvvvvvvvvvvvvveeeeee!"*

If I was going to go out, that would've been as good a way as any. Ending on love. What more could you ask?

Yelling over the applause, Randy said, "Yo, check it out, man, check it out, dog. I'm just keeping it real—you know the Dog always keeps it real—that was really just like karaoke, dude. Vocally, it wasn't really good at all." The audience booed him. (I loved those *Idol* studio audiences. They ruled.) "It was very bland and boring for me. I'm just being honest.

Come on. What're we doing up here? Paula, what're we doing?"

Paula chuckled. "Well, we're watching somebody who loves adversity. You thrive on it. You love it. Don't you?" I wondered if she knew about the "Mercedes Benz" fiasco, because that was adversity, and I definitely wasn't thriving. "You looked like you were having fun. But the vocals? Enh. You're a lovable guy, Sanjaya. You are." And that was it. Nothing constructive. Nothing positive. Oh, well.

Then Simon burst right in. "Utterly horrendous. Honestly, it was as bad as anything we see at the beginning of *American Idol*."

Enter the eternally kind Ryan Seacrest. "Simon, Simon, Simon, Simon, Simon," he groaned. "Even if it wasn't his best performance, you've never really liked this guy. So was it the song, or was it that you just don't like Sanjaya?"

Simon said, "Excuse me, who rattled your cage?" He motioned Ryan to move away from me, as if he was interrupting the proceedings. "To the left, to the left, to the left."

Ryan ignored him, then said, "Paula, if he came out here, and—"

Simon interrupted, "Oh, shut up, Ryan." Simon and Ryan picked on each other both on and off the air all the time, but to me, this was the first time it seemed like Simon was actually annoyed. "What I'm trying to say is, I know this has been funny for a while, but based on the fact that we are supposed to be finding an American idol . . . it was hideous. A ridiculous choice of song."

I wanted to yell out, "*Tell that to the producers!*" But I held my tongue.

Ryan said, "Randy, if Sanjaya ever really nailed it, would Simon like it?"

Not letting Randy get a word in edgewise, Simon said, "I liked him last week, big mouth."

Randy roared, "Yeah, he liked him last week."

And then Randy and Simon started yelling over each other, and nobody could understand a word they were saying. Finally, Paula raised her hands and said, "Okay, okay, enough, enough."

Thirty minutes later, I learned that that's what America said about me: *enough*. My premonition was right. I was cut.

It would be easy for me to blame country music, Ford Motors, Simon, or hotel air-conditioning for my exit, but honestly, I believe it was my time to go. My spirit was high after Latin Week, but once Country Week came around, it plummeted, and I wasn't able to amp it up again. I wanted to keep my energy and my focus, but I couldn't do it. Something was happening beyond my control, and I was too drained to even try to figure out what that something was. Only a handful of people in the entire world knew what it felt like to make it to the *American Idol* Top 10.

Melinda Doolittle

I loved it when he did "Let's Give Them Something to Talk About." To me, it felt like he was saying, "Let's give them something to talk about other than hair." That was the best Sanjaya move. I was so proud of him. What a way to go out. He mentioned to everybody that he thought he was going home, but nobody took him too seriously, because everybody always mentioned that they thought they were going home. Plus he was The Bounce-back Kid. I was shocked when he was gone.

Immediately after the show, I was taken into an office to speak with the *Idol* counselor, whose job it was to make sure that a contestant didn't harm himself after getting cut. A youngish woman in a pretty blue dress, she said, "Sanjaya, are you okay?"

I smiled. "Yeah. I'm fine. I'm cool."

She peered at me for what seemed like an hour, then said, "You're supposed to be upset."

"Nope. I'm cool."

"Well, I'm suspicious."

"You shouldn't be. I'm fine. I just had this incredible experience, and I got further than I ever could've imagined, and three months from now, I'm going on tour with a whole bunch of my friends. Really, I'm fine."

She peered at me again, right in the eyes. She must've liked what she saw, because she said, "You're right. You're fine. Good luck with everything."

After I said good-bye to all the backstage people and filled out a bunch of paperwork that I didn't really understand (or, right at that moment, care about), I did my exit interview for the *Idol* website with James Pumphrey.

James was a nice guy with a soothing vibe, which is important, because you don't want some loud journalist in your face right after all of America rejected you and your singing. "How're you doing?" he asked.

"Good. Better than I thought I would be."

"Good," he quietly said. "Now let's get right down to it. You definitely got a lot of criticism and praise, but a lot of people said that you didn't deserve to be here. Are you more surprised that you're gone, or are you more surprised that you made it to the Top Seven in spite of everything?"

Excellent question, I thought. *That's probably the same thing I would've asked myself.* "I think I was more surprised that I made it to Seven. Each week, I was just trying to be myself, trying to put myself out there and hope that America caught onto that. I made it to where I think I needed to put my message across. And I'm definitely not done. You're not going to see the last of me . . . unfortunately for some people. It's been a roller coaster, but it's the most fun roller coaster I've been on in a long, long time."

"Speaking of fun," James said, "when we came to the show beforehand, more than anybody, you were always smiling, and you always had a new hairdo, and you were always really excited. And more than anybody else, you got ridiculous criticism from the judges, to the point that Simon even gave up commenting on your vocals. How did you stay positive, in spite of so much negativity?"

Another good question, and I had to gather my thoughts for a second before I could answer. "I tried to turn the negatives into positives by taking anything I could learn from it. And if it was flat-out negative, I just left it. If you don't, you'll drive yourself crazy."

"What did you learn from this experience?"

That was easy. "I just learned to be myself. That's the most important thing you can do. You are always going to be you, even when people try to change you into what they want you to be. Really, it's easiest to be you." He then asked a few silly questions about my hair (of course), and then, after a few more press interviews, I went to my farewell party.

During the Top 10, after somebody was cut, we always had a roast-slash-good-bye-dinner for whoever was heading home. Being the kind of people we are, we always had less of a roast and more of a tribute, because we all honestly liked, respected, and cared for one another. We had honest, wholesome, loving relationships, and I'll always cherish that.

Phil Stacey

I've started up many little businesses, so I have an idea of how the industry works, and I looked at Sanjaya and thought that he has the ability to become humongous. I'm a guy who's spent five hundred dollars on tickets to the Wiggles for his daughters, and if Sanjaya goes into children's music, he could be right there.

After Blake, Chris Richardson, Jordin, LaKisha, and Melinda gave their little speeches, Phil stood up, looked around the room, and said, "We're here with six people who could potentially be millionaires." And then he put his arm around my shoulders, pulled me into an embrace, and said, "But we're also standing in the presence of a future billionaire."

Melinda Doolittle

I think Sanjaya could be great at anything he wanted to. If he put his mind to doing children's music, he'd be great at it. If he wanted to do subtle R & B grooves, he'd be amazing at that.

That made me feel *sooooooooooo* good, that a cool, talented guy like Phil Stacey would say that I have the potential to be successful at doing exactly what I want to do. All I could say was thank you.

Jordin Sparks

I got very emotional when he was cut, and I bawled my eyes out.
He was a part of me, and I was so sad. After he left, I didn't
know what to do with myself. That night, he came over to the
room with his guitar and sang "Landslide" by Fleetwood Mac.
I cried and cried and cried, and he kept saying, "It's okay, it's
okay, it's okay." And he was right. It was okay.

I headed back to the hotel, and as I was packing up my clothes, I thought about my last performance. As much as my heart wasn't into it, the Bonnie Raitt tune was the most appropriate thing I could've done as my swan song, because if nothing else, I gave *American Idol* fans lots of somethings to talk about: the hair, the clothes, and the whippings at the hands of the Big Three.

But I had to move forward. I couldn't look back.

I had to give them something *else* to talk about.

PART THREE

Who Is Bill Vendall?

The online video post started off with a clip of my worst vocal moment on *American Idol*: my somewhat out-of-tune entrance on "Cheek to Cheek." And then it cut to a title card:

THE SANJAYA INSTALLATION

Next, you see me sitting on a sofa, dressed in all black and wearing a pair of oversize, white-rimmed sunglasses. I look directly at the camera and speak:

"Good afternoon. I'm Bill Vendall, a twenty-five-year-old graduate student in the industrial design program at RISD. For the past five months, I've assumed the role of a character I'd created named Sanjaya Malakar. The character was part of a larger art installation for my thesis program. To the fans of Sanjaya—maybe you're actually a fan of Bill Vendall, the artist. I'm sure many of you subconsciously knew what I was doing. How could you look at this"—you then see, in quick succession, photos of all my hairdos—"and not see it as a symbol for the self-referencing nature of progressive evolution. This won't be the last you see of me. I might show up in other places. I might pop up on your favorite situation comedy. I might run for president. I might show up as . . . *you*."

This little one-minute video spread through cyberspace like a virus, and *American Idol* fans freaked out. Was there really a Sanjaya? Did I manage to fool the entire *Idol* research department? Is this book you're holding in your hands a complete hoax?

Nah. It was just a little somethin'-somethin' I filmed for Will Ferrell's website funnyordie.com the afternoon after I was cut. I guess I was more or less in a pretty good space. Granted, I didn't have the kind of mind-set where I could take stock in myself, or try to figure out where I was headed. I had a one-step-at-a-time attitude about the whole thing, and step one was dealing with the media.

Press Week

Yes, I was in a pretty good headspace, but there was a part of me that was a little bit sad that I was done, mostly because I'd miss the camaraderie—but there was the *Idol* tour to look forward to, which would give us all plenty of time to hang. (Chris Sligh, Haley, and Gina, the three Top 10 people who got cut before I did, would be back in the fold, and that was going to be awesome.) But mostly, I was relieved. Yes, *Idol* was fun and fulfilling, but in the end, the intensity got to be a bit overwhelming. I'm glad I did it, but knowing what I know now, I wouldn't do it again.

Just because you're through on the show doesn't mean you're through with *American Idol*. In some ways, you work harder the week after you've been cut than you had during any week prior. With the show itself, you fall into a routine: you solidify your song choice, you rehearse with the pianist, you meet the mentor, you go to dress rehearsal, you do the live show, you get told by Simon Cowell how dreadful you are, and then you do it again. Yes, there's a lot of rushing around that leads into mind-numbing downtime, and yes, you don't eat well, and yes, you don't get enough sleep, but at least you know what's coming next, what to expect, what's around the corner.

Press Week, however, is a different story. I wasn't even given any time to rest and recover; a mere eighteen hours after I was cut, I was a guest on *The Tonight Show with Jay Leno*. Talk about no rest for the weary. But it was cool, because I was a huge Leno fan. No, check that: it was *really* cool.

None of the other contestants who'd been cut had done Leno, so I didn't know what to expect. I assumed that I'd be just like any other musical guest: sing my song, talk to Jay for three seconds, then go onto the next stop. Wrong. They wanted me to appear in a sketch, and then have Jay grill me at the desk. No singing, just talking.

My sketch was right after Jay's monologue. They started it off by running the video of Ryan telling me that I was going home, then they cut right back to Jay, who said, "We felt bad for Sanjaya—he's going to be on later as a guest—so I wanted to bring him out now. So from Seattle, Washington, please welcome Sanjaya Malakar."

I stepped out from the backstage area, surprised at how tiny the studio was. I shook hands with Jay, who then said, "Sanjaya is a real *American Idol* contestant, but not yet a real pop idol. So to help tell his story, we hired a real teen pop idol, Donny Osmond." After the warm applause died down,

Jay said, "Sanjaya, you captured the imagination of the American public. What is it about you that people find so fascinating?"

I was having a mild freak-out, because I had to read the teleprompter and look like I *wasn't* reading the teleprompter, which is definitely not as easy as it sounds. "I don't know," I said. "Maybe it's because I'm young, or because I take risks, or because I like having fun." And then Donny broke in with a bastardizing of the song "Hair" (and that's "Hair" as in "Gimme a head with hair / Long beautiful hair"), which ended with him singing "Ponytail, Mohawk, faux-haux," and offering up a little raspberry.

I knew it was coming, but I still cracked up; Donny Osmond was a funny dude. Jay then asked me, "What about that young girl in the audience who was crying for you?"

I said, "I have lots of young fans, and I'm happy they like my singing." Donny then sang a snatch of his biggest hit, "Puppy Love."

Jay said, "One last question: You spend a lot of time with Ryan Seacrest. What was the last thing you said to him?"

I said, "I told him that I really appreciated his support." And then Donny sang, "Go Away Little Girl." And that was funny, but I've said it before and I'll say it again: *Ryan Seacrest is not gay. Ask his girlfriend. She'll tell you.*

Twenty minutes later, after actor/singer/Tenacious D co-leader Jack Black—who apparently is a regular viewer of *American Idol*—gave a hilarious interview, Jay introduced me, and out I went. I was a little nervous, because this was my first talk show appearance, but I knew I'd better get at it, because there were plenty more to come. It didn't help that I was sitting in between two guys I thought were superfunny, Jay Leno and Jack Black. To repeat: *I was sitting in between Leno and*

Jack Black. I'm not the sort of person who gets starstruck, but I'll admit that that was pretty awesome. In a way, it calmed me down, because I knew that if I stumbled, these guys would pick me up.

After I told Jay that I felt okay about being cut, he asked me, "Are you hard on yourself? Or do you just have a good time, whatever it is?"

I said, "I just have a good time, and I try to learn from every experience that I have, so it's cool."

And then Jack Black busted in with his Jack Blacky voice: "You had a great *riiiiiiiide*, Sanjayaaaaaaaa. I was rooting for you. I didn't vote, but if I had voted, I would've absolutely voted for you. Actually I would've voted for the chubby dude"—I assumed he meant Chris Sligh—"and then you, and then a couple others I'm not going to say."

Jay asked Jack, "Why the chubby dude?"

Jack said, "I felt the kinship. Plus one time he gave me a shout-out. He said he was a combo of me and Jack Osbourne. Jack Black Osbourne." (Thinking about it, I realized that Chris was right—he *was* a combination of Jack Black and Jack Osbourne.) Jack Black is way funnier than I'll ever be, and I didn't mind at all that he was taking up my interview time.

Jay did, however, so he asked me, "You've gone from nobody knowing you to the entire nation talking about you in a short amount of time, and I thought you handled it quite well. Some people, their head gets a lot bigger." *Wow, I* thought, *all these stars are being cool to me!* Unbelievable. He continued, "What's it like being judged like that all the time?"

I don't know why, but I kind of froze up. After ten seconds of repeating "I . . . I . . . I . . . I . . ." I was finally able to get a coherent thought across: "It's crazy. I'm just a kid from Seattle. I'm not a"—and then I did some finger quotes—"celebrity."

Jack, who practically had his arm around me, said, "You are now, baby."

"Yeah," I said, "it's really weird."

"That is weird," Jack said. "Two months ago, not at all. Now you're as famous as you can be."

Then Jay said, "And you have fan-jayas."

I said, "Fan-jayas who have been Sanjaya'ed."

Jay asked, "What does that mean if you've been Sanjaya'ed?"

"I don't know. I thought Sanjaya was a verb. I didn't know nouns could become verbs." *Not bad*, I thought. *I'm being kind of funny on* The Tonight Show.

And then he asked the question that I'll probably be asked for the rest of my life: "What about Simon? He was pretty hard on you. Did it ever sting a little?"

"No. I think he saw some potential in me, and I never lived up to it."

Jack said, "Seemed like he was mad at you. Seemed like he was going after you extra. He put a little extra paprika on his insults. I was like, *What's up, dude? Lay off of the Sanjaya.*"

The interview lasted a couple more minutes, my favorite moment being when I told Jay I was half Italian, and he said, "Ah, he's Italian. I knew there was a reason I loved this kid," and then Jack shouted out, "*Hey, India's rad too!*" I thought, *Oh my gosh, they're talking about me!* Too weird.

Jay finished up by asking me if I'd voted for myself. When I told him I voted for the other contestants, he said, "So you're an honorable person. And you want to be in showbiz. Those two things don't mix."

I knew Jay was joking. But I hoped he was wrong.

The next day, it was Ellen DeGeneres, who was just as sweet as you'd think she'd be. Her energy is warm and cool, and it's refreshing to go on a show like that and act like a celebrity without feeling weird. (Okay, I wasn't a real celebrity; I was just a kid who was more of a pseudo-celebrity.) The person you see on TV is the person you see in person. That's something I'll always strive for—to keep grounded, real, and true to myself.

Ellen gave me, as an arrival gift, some boxers with her show's logo on the front, and a big, white, fuzzy, plushy bathrobe, the softest robe I'd ever worn. For the show, I wanted to wear the boxers over my pants, and then put the robe on, but Mom wouldn't let me, because she wanted to make sure that I came across as somewhat serious. I said, "Come on, Mom, it's *Ellen*. She's cool." I got vetoed.

After I was introduced—to a standing ovation, which was unexpected and weird—I sat down next to Ellen, and the first thing she said to me was, "We have a crying girl in the audience. Did you see her?"

I did. But it wasn't Ashley Ferl, just one of Ellen's blond-haired staffers, doing a nice job of fake-bawling. After the interview was over, I ran out into the audience and gave her a big old hug . . . and then started fake—making out with her. (I hoped Ashley wasn't watching.) Later on, Ellen told me that she was a big fan of mine. I thanked her, then said, "I'm a fan of yours. It doesn't go the other way. I'm the fan. I watch you on TV all the time."

At six o'clock the next morning, I was out of the hotel and on a plane to New York. I'd spent a little bit of time in New York with my family, but only as a total tourist. We rode around Central Park in a horse-driven carriage, went to the top of the Statue of Liberty, and hit Times Square. I could envision myself living there someday. The West Coast is more laid-back, go-with-the-flow, and the East Coast is all energy. There's a flow to go with in New York, but it's a lot faster, and I liked it.

My schedule was so insane that I had to flow even faster than everybody else. The first place I flowed to was the Ed Sullivan Theater, home of *Late Show with David Letterman*.

I liked Letterman as much as I did Leno, and I generally picked which show to watch based on the musical guest. (Like if Dave had on a country singer, I'd watch Jay, and vice versa.) I was a huge fan of his Top Ten lists, so when they asked me to read it that night, I was thrilled.

Dave said, "The category tonight: top ten things I learned from *American Idol*." He paused, then said, "I'll just say one thing about *American Idol*: I'm a big supporter of the show, I love the program, and I'll tell you why. The United States is facing a serious superstar shortage, and this is the only way we're going to be able to replenish that treasure trove. At one time, we dominated the world with superstars. Not so now. And now, here to present your Top Ten list, your latest *American Idol* castoff, Sanjaya Malaker, ladies and gentlemen."

Unlike with my sketch on Leno, I didn't have to worry about looking like I wasn't reading the teleprompter, so I wasn't nearly as nervous. And as usual, the list was awesome:

10. *The camera adds ten pounds to your Mohawk.*
9. *Work hard and make sacrifices, and you can finish in seventh place.*
8. *It's very important to "keep it real, dawg."*
7. *I should've gone for the immunity idol . . . oh, wait, that's* Survivor.

6. On camera, Simon's a bit nasty, but off camera, he's a total jerk.

5. Voting for yourself a hundred times an hour causes some wicked carpal tunnel.

4. When you forget the words, just do this: "Ohhh-hhh oooohhhh aawwwww, yes he did."

3. Honestly, I thought I was auditioning for Are You Smarter Than a 5th Grader?

2. Nothing.

1. America loves performers with bad hair—right, Dave?

Dave laughed, people clapped, I had a great time, the energy was really chill, and the whole thing felt great. He wasn't *David Letterman*; he was just some dude who had a TV show that I was on, and if for some reason I ever have a talk show, I'll do everything I can to make my guests feel equally comfortable.

I was looking forward to chilling out and watching the rest of the show, so I gave the stagehand my collar microphone and headed back to the dressing room. Thirty seconds later, the stagehand came scrambling over, shoved the mic into my hand, and said, "They want you back out there. Hurry. Hurry!"

Turns out Dave wanted me to sing my "*Ohhhhhh oooohhhh aawwwwww, yes he did*" again, and I was happy to oblige. (Note: I stole the "*Ohhhhhh oooohhhh aawwwwww, yes he did*" from one Melinda Doolittle. Obviously, she does it *way* better than I do.) As I was walking off, I heard Dave say, "He seems a little too comfortable here. Twice, he didn't want to leave."

And then Paul Shaffer, Dave's eternal bandleader, said, "Where else does he have to go?"

Well, I thought, *dinner for a start*.

I'm not a morning person, but I somehow managed to pull it together the next day for an early appearance on *The Today Show*, which turned out to be a good cop–bad cop situation. Meredith Vieira lobbed me the softball questions: how was I feeling, was I okay going home, how did I deal with Simon, and so on. And then Matt Lauer—who always seemed like a nice guy to me—said, "I'm going to be very honest, Sanjaya, because honesty is the best policy: I don't watch the show, but when I'd see the clips, I'd question whether your talent was at the same level as the other people's, and I even said it on the air. When you went onto the competition, and you first saw yourself in the group of twenty, how did you rate your talent as compared to theirs?"

Wow. A *totally* loaded question. I tried to be as honest as possible: "I didn't think I was the best singer on the show, but I think that we were each unique, and that's what makes the show so awesome, and such a phenomenon. It's not about who's the best. It's about who makes people feel their music the most."

Matt said, "Or who gets people talking."

The next day, I had perhaps my strangest talk show appearance on a local New York show called *The Morning Show with Mike and Juliet*, where, right before the show, they sprung Ashley Ferl the Crying Girl and her entire family on me. I didn't mind seeing her, but my publicist freaked out. It was okay that she was there, but it would've been nice to have some advance notice.

Naturally, she started bawling, and naturally, they brought her up onstage. Juliet, who had some impressive hair herself, said to Ashley, "When I first saw you, I was crying for you . . . and I'm an adult. So I don't understand this. Is it just that you have a crush on him? Or do you want to be like him? Why do you think you're crying?"

"I don't *knnnnnnnnnnooooooooooowwww*." Ashley could barely get the words out.

Juliet turned to me. "Is this funny? Does this crack you up? Or does it touch your heart?"

I answered, "It touches my heart. I've never had someone cry over me."

Juliet said, "Awwwwww," then went back to Ashley. "What do you want to do with your life? I heard you wanted to be on *American Idol*."

Ashley still couldn't really speak, so I gave her an encouraging round of applause and said, "Do it, do it!" She giggled and squirmed, and it was then that I noticed her T-shirt.

So did Juliet. "Oh my God, look at that shirt. There are Sanjayas everywhere." Sure enough, there were nine pictures of me arranged in a grid. "I think she's got every hairdo there."

Compared to the twelve-year-old boy who followed me through Manhattan that week, Ashley and her family were a pleasure. I'd spotted him by the *Letterman* studio, but then he showed up at *Mike and Juliet*, which I thought was a bit strange. He approached me and said, "Can I have your autograph, Sanjaya?"

I said yes, because I'll pretty much give *anybody* an autograph. I always sign using a blue pen, because my publicist told me that if you use black, intrepid autograph freaks can pull your signature off the page and use it anywhere: to sell on eBay, or to trade for other autographs, or, worst of all, to cash a check. He handed me a black pen, but I had a blue pen in my pocket. I said, "Haven't I seen you before?"

He ignored my question. "Can I have your autograph?"

My publicist whispered into my ear, "Don't sign. He's paparazzi."

"He's, like, twelve," I whispered back.

"I've seen him around. Don't sign. Let's go."

So I'm sitting in the car, and he was sprinting alongside us, banging on the window like the little beggar kids in India, dodging fast-moving cars and pedestrians, all the while yelling, "Please let me have your autograph! Please! Please! Please!"

I said, "Sorry, I can't." I turned to my publicist and said, "I'd like to sign something for him in silver pen"—which would make it impossible for him to do anything with—"and write, 'You have a great future as a sprinter.' "

The next morning, it was time for my meeting with Rachael Ray. I love the Food Network, and I love cooking, but unfortunately, they didn't want me on the show for my culinary skills. The vibe in her studio is as mellow as it is in Letterman's, but in a more feminine way, which makes sense, because practically everybody in the audience was female.

The first thing she said was, "Sanjaya was a little late getting to the studio because he was being chased by paparazzi. What's that like?"

I said, "It's freaky. I'm still just Sanjaya from Seattle, and I wouldn't think that people would even care to chase me. It really feels kind of unnatural."

Rachael, who I should note is supercute and supersweet, asked, "How's it been for you? I mean, you're in this position where you have millions of legitimate fans, and all of these little girls chasing you everywhere, and then you have this whole other weird counterculture movement of people screaming, *Get him off, we think he's the worst!* How are you dealing with that?"

I'd only been off the show for a few days, and I'd already been asked that question in one form or another at least twenty times, but I thought Rachael did a great job of wording it. I said, "I just didn't focus on the negative. I think the most important thing you can do is stay positive, and just learn from everything."

As the crowd applauded, she said, "I remember that that's what Tony Bennett said he loved most about you, that you're a real individual, and he thought you had a lot of great panache. Now, you've met some huge icons in music, and I'm sure you've learned a lot just from chatting with them. Is there anyone between the great Gwen Stefani, and Tony Bennett, and J.Lo who gave you one piece of advice where you were like. *Wow, that's something I can really hang on to?*"

I was surprised and pleased about how well this was going. Rachael was known as a cook, so I wasn't sure what to expect. But she was asking me more thoughtful questions than Matt Lauer, whom many consider to be one of the best interviewers in the world. "I think when Jennifer Lopez told the whole cast to really feel the music, and listen to the lyrics and really connect to them, that's the most important thing for a performer to do. Because if the audience doesn't feel what you're saying, they're going to disconnect."

Rachael said, "I think that was where you really handled yourself with a ton of class. You tried to be a great entertainer every week. So I want to know what life is like being part of that show on a day-to-day basis. What's it like behind the scenes there?"

I couldn't give as extensive an answer as she would've liked, because before the show starts filming, all *American Idol* contestants sign a nondisclosure agreement saying that we're not allowed to discuss anything too in-depth about the show for one full year. If you make the Top 3, however, that extends to five years. All of which meant I had to speak in generalities: "It's very stressful," I said. "You don't have time to do anything else other than the show."

I think Rachael knew she wasn't going to get any great revelations, so she said, "It's a grind. Not only are you trying to prepare to perform, but you're literally going around the clock. Maybe that was the toughest part, you think?"

I told her that the toughest part was picking songs, but I obviously didn't mention anything about the "Mercedes Benz" fiasco, as much as I wanted to. But those nondisclosures are pretty airtight, so why take a chance?

Press Week ended right back where it started, in Los Angeles, with a visit to *Jimmy Kimmel*.

"He has a head of hair so shiny and luscious that it carried him all the way to the finals of *American Idol*. He's here tonight to show it to us—and perhaps even let us touch it." And he started in on me right away. "It's weird to meet you, because I've been watching you on television, and you almost tore this nation apart. Did you have any intention of doing that? Was that a goal of yours?" I tried to say something, but then he bulled in: "No, you had no idea." He then started asking me the typical Press Week questions, which I'd grown tired of, but I was always happy to answer. But then he came up with something funny: "Do you get the sense that the other contestants were voting for themselves?" I gave him a little mumble of assent, then he said, "Oh, really? Who do you think is doing this? Can you give us a hint? The bald guy?" I hoped Phil Stacey was watching; he'd probably appreciate being called "the Bald Guy" by Jimmy Kimmel. "Do you think he felt jealous of your hair and thought, 'I've got to do something'?" I shrugged. "You don't know. Well, I've suspected him of wrongdoing. Well, you didn't vote for yourself. That's something. I definitely would've voted for myself. I apologize: I only voted for you about three hundred times. I feel like I didn't hold up my end. What's the biggest number you've heard?"

Wow, I thought, *I finally get to say something.* "My aunt voted for me eleven hundred times. She called in with three phones."

"Do you know if your sister voted for you?" I shook my head. "You've got to find out who voted for you, and if they didn't, you should destroy them. This is important, that you figure out who your alliances are, and who you can't trust anymore. Also, if she goes next year, and she's in the final twenty-four you shouldn't vote for her if she didn't vote for you."

Jimmy Kimmel is a funny guy, but man, can he talk.

As for me, I was talked out. It was time to go home.

Back in Seattle

Even though I'd been out of commission for only six or so months, I thought I would feel like a different person, more mature, more worldly, more *everything*. But only a few days after slipping back into my old Seattle life, I realized that I was the same old Sanjaya, the only change being that I was a better performer than I was when I left, and I'd been on television a few times.

I felt like some people in my situation might be concerned about how they were perceived by their people at home, but I wasn't worried what anybody thought about me. I never felt like I needed to impress people, either before or after the show. I was always going to be me, and if somebody liked me, great, but if not, I'd go on with my life, and there were plenty of other public figures—or even *American Idol* contestants—for them to blog about.

So yes, I was the same, but that surprised my friends and family, most of whom treated me differently during my week at home before the *Idol* tour. Members of my extended family hit me up for signed pictures, and my little cousins asked me, "Are you a rock star? I want to be a rock star too." Another oddity: all of my younger boy cousins had grown their hair out, and some of them constantly asked for advice on hairstyles. I just prayed there wouldn't be a rash of ponyhawks.

A couple of my friends also expected a new Sanjaya. "Why aren't you different?" they'd ask. "I was watching you on TV, and here you are, and you're the exact same person."

I'd say, "Um, yeah. Did you not know me as well as I thought you did before I left?"

I guess that was the most surprising and disappointing thing, the fact that both family and friends were projecting things on me that weren't there. Did they want me to come home in a limo, all covered in bling, wearing a three-thousand-dollar Hugo Boss suit? Didn't they watch me on the talk shows? I wore T-shirts and jeans, same as I always did. It was all kind of isolating, but I only had a short time at home before it was back to Los Angeles to finish out my commitment to *American Idol*: an appearance on the final show, where Jordin Sparks deservedly won; many, many rehearsals; and the launch of a grueling fifty-six-concert tour, where I'd find out if I had the heart and stamina to have a career in music.

But I figured that if I made it through *Idol* with my sanity, I'd be okay on the road, because the pressure of competing would be gone.

Little did I know.

The Tour

Hollywood Week was really, really hard.

The Top 10 was really really, really hard.

The *American Idol* 2007 summer tour was so hard that a zillion reallys would just start to scratch the surface. When I was handed the itinerary . . .

- July 6: Sunrise, FL—BankAtlantic Center
- July 7: Tampa, FL—St. Pete Times Forum
- July 8: Jacksonville, FL—Jacksonville Veterans Memorial Arena
- July 10: Greenville, SC—BI-LO Center
- July 11: Nashville, TN—Nashville Arena
- July 12: Birmingham, AL—BJCC Arena

- July 13: N. Little Rock, AR—Alltel Arena
- July 15: Houston, TX—Toyota Center
- July 16: San Antonio, TX—AT&T Center
- July 18: Glendale, AZ—Jobing.com Arena
- July 19: San Diego, CA—San Diego Sports Arena
- July 20: Fresno, CA—Save Mart Center
- July 22: Anaheim, CA—Honda Center
- July 23: Los Angeles, CA—STAPLES Center
- July 24: San Jose, CA—HP Pavilion at San Jose
- July 25: Sacramento, CA—ARCO Arena
- July 27: Tacoma, WA—Tacoma Dome
- July 28: Portland, OR—Rose Garden
- July 30: Nampa, ID—Idaho Center
- July 31: Salt Lake City, UT—EnergySolutions Arena
- August 3: Omaha, NE—Qwest Center
- August 4: St. Paul, MN—Xcel Energy Center
- August 5: Milwaukee, WI—Bradley Center
- August 7: Rosemont, IL—Allstate Arena
- August 8: Moline, IL—MARK of the Quad Cities
- August 9: St. Louis, MO—Scottrade Center
- August 11: Columbus, OH—Schottenstein Center
- August 12: Auburn Hills, MI—Palace of Auburn Hills
- August 13: Cleveland, OH—Wolstein Center
- August 14: Toronto, ON—Air Canada Centre
- August 16: Indianapolis, IN—Indiana State Fair
- August 17: Louisville, KY—Kentucky State Fair
- August 18: Sedalia, MO—Missouri State Fair

- August 19: Des Moines, IA—Iowa State Fair
- August 22: Pittsburgh, PA—Mellon Arena
- August 23: Rochester, NY—Blue Cross Arena
- August 24: Long Island, NY—Nassau Coliseum
- August 27: Hartford, CT—Hartford Civic Center
- August 28: E. Rutherford, NJ—Continental Airlines Arena
- August 30: Albany, NY—Times Union Center
- September 1: Allentown, PA—Allentown Fair
- September 2: Syracuse, NY—New York State Fair
- September 4: Portland, ME—Cumberland County Civic Center
- September 5: Worcester, MA—DCU Center
- September 7: Philadelphia, PA—Wachovia Center
- September 8: Atlantic City, NJ—Boardwalk Hall
- September 9: Washington, DC—Verizon Center
- September 11: Greensboro, NC—Greensboro Coliseum
- September 12: Duluth, GA—Arena at Gwinnett Center
- September 13: Memphis, TN—FedEx Forum
- September 15: Huntington, WV—Big Sandy Super-store Arena
- September 16: Charlottesville, VA—John Paul Jones Arena
- September 18: Hampton, VA—Hampton Coliseum
- September 19: Baltimore, MD—1st Mariner Arena
- September 20: Bridgeport, CT—Arena at Harbor Yard
- September 22: Manchester, NH—Verizon Wireless Arena

. . . I freaked. I knew to expect a lot of performances, but seeing fifty-six shows over two and a half months in black-and-white brought things crashing home.

The Los Angeles rehearsals kicked off almost immediately after Jordin was crowned the 2007 American Idol, and those sessions were a ton of fun—or at least they were for me, because I'd had a week to get my head together in Seattle. Most of the other nine singers in the crew had been running around the entire time, so I was one of the more rested people there, which was a relief, because we were worked *hard*. We spent as much time on the show's logistics—song selection, running order, choreography, clothing—as we did on singing, but that wasn't a surprise. As we'd all learned so well, that's the overriding message of *American Idol*: it's about the entire package.

After way too much discussion, we decided to open with "Let's Get It Started" by Black Eyed Peas. (Chris Richardson and Phil rapped the verses on that one. I think people were surprised at how well they did, probably because they both look pretty darn white.) Everybody performed one solo song, except for the first and second finishers, Jordin and Blake, who were, understandably enough, asked to do some extra material. For my solo tune, I picked Michael Jackson's "The Way You Make Me Feel"—just about as far removed from me as the first solo feature of my career, "Swing Low, Sweet Chariot," as you could get—partly because it was a ton of fun to sing, and partly because I figured it would get the crowd totally hyped. I mean, who doesn't get hyped about old-school stuff from the King of Pop?

Melinda Doolittle

Sanjaya really came out of his shell on tour. Jordin and I would be backstage listening to him sing "The Way You Make Me Feel," and watch him run across the stage, and the audiences just couldn't take it. They were screaming their heads off the entire time. I was excited that people were getting to see that side of him. I'd always introduce him by saying that his hair was better than any of my wigs. His hair would always be blowing in this wind that seemed to follow him anywhere.

For my group tunes, I dueted with Melinda on "Proud Mary," which was a treat because, well, singing with Melinda was *always* a treat. And Haley, Chris Richardson, and I decided to go with "Life Is a Highway" by Rascal Flatts, a southern blues rocker that I wish I knew about on Country Week. I will admit that I was skeptical about that one, because Chris Richardson, while he's an R & B singer, has a really good country voice, and Haley sings a ton of country; when I was asked to join them, I said, "Okay, I'll do it, and I'll do my best, but I don't know if I'm going to necessarily add anything to the song." One night in Michigan, I missed my cue, and the two of them ended up singing it as a duet. They were lovely. I don't think I was missed.

Melinda Doolittle

My favorite thing was when I called my mother and said, "I'm singing 'Proud Mary,' and I'm doing it as a duet with Sanjaya, and he rips off the bottom of my dress." She said, "I'm sorry? Is that legal?" We had a couple of nights where the dress was on wrong, so he'd go to rip it off and it wouldn't come off. It was a legitimate wardrobe malfunction.

After two weeks of prepping in L.A., we relocated to Florida for a round of rehearsals that would take us up to our first show. We kept working hard to nail down our numerous costume changes, dance steps, and vocal arrangements, but we realized that no matter how much or how well we readied ourselves for the show, there was no such thing as perfection on our stages once the shows started. None of the venues were laid out the same, and since all we did were one-nighters, there was never a chance for the technical people to get comfortable. No matter how hard we mapped things out, there were going to be foul-ups that were beyond our control.

That being the case, we all slacked off on some stuff. Much of the choreography went out the window after the second week, and about 60 percent of the costumes weren't seen after week three. Set lists changed (Melinda and Blake's version of "Killing Me Softly" got axed early on, as did Chris Sligh's take on "Another One Bites the Dust"), lighting was altered, and the rear projection screens sometimes didn't get set up . . . but we never got any complaints. I was working with a bunch of talented people, and they were going to put on a good show no matter what.

Phil Stacey

Sanjaya was one of the top entertainers on the tour. He always put on a great show. It was always one of the highlights for the crowd. Every night he came out and nailed it. Of course, we had monitors, so we all sounded better.

No matter how much we messed up, at least we all looked good . . . or at least sort of good. Our stylist came from Broadway, and some of what she concocted was kind of overly theatrical, not as good as it potentially could've been. I like to think I have an eye for that sort of thing, and I used to look at Jordin, Gina, and Haley and think, *They look great, but they could look so much better.* For instance, during the final number, everybody wore random all-white outfits, while Jordin wore a sparkly silver dress with an out-of-place bow on the back that didn't fit her as well as it should've. From the front of the house, it looked fine, but from our view behind her, it looked too big. I'd always stare at Jordin and think, *You look pretty, but . . . let's go shopping!*

So we hit the mall, and right away I spotted a pretty black dress that I knew would work. Jordin wasn't into it, but I wasn't going to let it go. I started pestering her: "Come on, come on, try it on, try it on, come on, try it on, do it, do it, just humor me." I eventually wore her down, and when she came out of the dressing room . . . *perfection.* It was just the right size to show off all her best features—she's curvy, she has boobs—and it made her look beautiful. It became her dress for the closing number for the rest of the tour.

Jordin Sparks

On tour, there wasn't a curfew, so everybody could go out and do whatever they wanted, which usually involved going to a club, and obviously Sanjaya and I couldn't go because we were underage, so we'd hang out together and talk until five in the morning. Sometimes we'd fall asleep next to each other on the bed, then wake up a few hours later and go, "Ahhhhhh! What're you doing here?!" And then we'd order room service together. One morning, we ordered every breakfast on the menu and ate it all. Sanjaya may be skinny, but he can eat like no other. And he's the kind of guy who doesn't exercise at all, then does twenty sit-ups a night for a week and ends up with washboard abs. That is so not fair.

The shows themselves were almost always solid—aside from the time I missed a cue, but we won't talk about that anymore, because I got yelled at really badly, and discussing it brings back bad memories—but the in-between stuff was sometimes difficult. You might think that traveling on a fancy tour bus would be glamorous; truthfully, it's anything but. There's no privacy, the only place you can stretch out is in your bunk—which is the size and shape of a coffin—and there isn't much to do except read, listen to music, and play video games. (Fortunately, the guys all got along really well, so there were very few squabbles or arguments on the boys' bus; I can't speak to what happened with the girls.)

Another problem: we were *always* tired. Some of our drives were twelve, fourteen, sixteen hours long, and on those nights, we'd either sleep in the bus or stumble into a hotel at four in the morning, only to have to wake up three hours later for an interview, an autograph session, or a meet-and-greet. Sometimes there wasn't enough time to clean up at the hotel, so we'd have to shower at the venue, which meant standing in a nasty athlete's-foot shower stall. Okay, I'll admit that the venues were more sanitary than the indie clubs back home in Seattle, but it still wasn't pleasant.

Phil Stacey

You're going to get people who change a little bit, but even the people who changed recognized that they were changing, and immediately went around and apologized to everybody. Everybody checked themselves.

As was the case when we were doing the TV show, Jordin and I spent a lot of time together because of our age. We didn't have a curfew, but when the other eight would hit the clubs, we couldn't go. No fake IDs for Jordin Sparks and Sanjaya Malakar, thank you very much. We were each other's confidants, and she used me as a sounding board for her boy problems. Her main issue was that she thought Chris Richardson was cute, and she wished that she were older so maybe they could date. I thought that was *soooooo* cute, and truthfully, I could totally understand why she had a crush on him: Chris was a gentleman, and good-looking, and nice, and funny, and talented . . . but he was twenty-three, and she was seventeen. Six years difference isn't a big deal when you're both in your twenties, but Jordin was fresh out of high school, and Chris wasn't. I knew that Jordin wanted me to tell Chris that she liked him, so I was kind of the monkey in the middle—or the love monkey in the middle, if you will. It was all very high school. Again I was the floater, going between the upstairs kids and the downstairs kids, so it was very familiar.

Jordin Sparks

I talked to him about boys all the time. I mean, I could talk to Melinda about stuff, but to get a guy's perspective was awesome.

If I learned one thing during this tour, it was that the saying "Patience is a virtue" is truer than you could ever imagine. The hurry-up-and-wait aspect of the *American Idol* television show is a fraction of what it is on the *American Idol* tour, so if you want to stay sane, you have to know how to chill. I also learned to take my fun where I could get it, and that you can't let any of life's stupid stuff affect your performance. When you're on tour, your life is all about staying focused and healthy for those 120 minutes onstage. Nothing else matters. Or at least nothing else *should* matter.

I didn't know what to expect when I first jumped onto the *American Idol* roller-coaster ride; honestly, I don't think *anybody* could've possibly guessed what they were in for. I grew to appreciate the craftsmanship it takes to go out and do the exact same show night after night, and the energy you need to make sure that the people who'd paid up to two hundred dollars a ticket got their money's worth. And best of all, I walked away with an internal book of music industry knowledge that it takes many musicians a lifetime of touring and recording to acquire.

Jordin Sparks

From watching the seasons before us, it seemed to me that they weren't as close as we were, although I don't want to speak for them, because I don't want anybody to get mad. But we got so incredibly close. We wanted to go out together, and talk constantly. I know that if I ever called Sanjaya, or Melinda, or Gina, or Chris Richardson, or Blake, or anybody, and I needed something, they'd be right there for me, and I'd do the same for them.

An End and a Beginning

I knew it was coming.

I knew it would be over before it started.

I knew that once the tour was completed, *American Idol* was going to wash its hands of me.

All the press I had gotten for them, and all the television interviews I'd done, and all the live concerts I'd performed on practically no sleep meant nothing. Their attitude was, *Season six is done. On to season seven. No looking back. Don't call us, we'll call you.*

Here's the deal: if you're an *Idol* Top 2 finalist, you are obligated to sign a management deal with 19 Entertainment, Simon "The Other Simon" Fuller's management company, and they have the right of first refusal with everybody else.

Well, they refused me.

On one level, I wasn't surprised. Simon Fuller headed up 19, but Simon Cowell probably carried some weight there, and we all know how Mr. Cowell felt about my singing. But because of what I'd learned on the show, I thought I'd become a pretty good entertainer (so did Randy Jackson and Paula Abdul; Simon Cowell, not so much, although he was coming around), and after the tour, I thought I was even better. I'd grown as a musician and an artist, and I'd just turned eighteen, so it was all but inevitable that I was going to grow some more. After all, practice makes perfect.

Nobody expected me to make it past Hollywood Week, let alone to the Top 10. And now, 19 Entertainment clearly didn't expect me to do anything. But as I'd proven over the previous months, I was all about defying expectations. You'd think that 19 Entertainment would have realized that and given me a shot.

But they didn't. And I was on my own.

And when did they drop the bombshell? Where did they tell me that they were dumping me as if I were a husband who got busted cheating on his spouse?

They didn't. I overheard a couple of contestants talking about it outside a fairgrounds in Louisville, Kentucky. Great way to celebrate the midpoint of a tour, right?

On the plus side, even if I did get signed, I'd be right in the middle of the heap: Jordin would be their first priority, then Blake, not to mention Kelly Clarkson, and Chris Daughtry, and all the other past *Idol* heavies. Also, not being tied to 19 Entertainment for five or six years (or five or six albums) meant that I had the freedom to map out the next phase of my career. This also meant I wouldn't have any commitments after we wrapped up the concerts, so I spent many hours on the tour bus planning what I was going to do when I got back to Seattle. Sleep was high on the list—I'd been overwhelmingly tired ever since the Green Mile—as was chilling with my friends, and hanging out with my family in a setting that didn't involve schedules, television cameras, or interviews. But mostly, I wanted to go somewhere where I wouldn't have to talk about *American Idol*, or Simon, or concerts, or showbiz. I figured that heading to the other side of the globe would be the right move.

Melinda Doolittle

When it's over, they move onto the next season immediately. They're just gone. That process can be really, really hard. I lived in Nashville, which is Music City, so I knew I could go home and find people to work with, but Sanjaya didn't have that. After Idol, lots of opportunities come your way, but what do you choose? What is it you want to do? It's hard for people like Sanjaya and me, because we went into Idol not really knowing what we wanted out of it. So when we got out of it, we were like, Uh-oh. Now I have to figure out what to do, and what I really love. It's definitely a journey.

So ten days after I got home, Shyamali and I packed our bags and went to New Zealand.

I've always had a weird connection with New Zealand ever since I saw the movie *Whale Rider*, a drama set and filmed on the country's coast. Aside from the fact that it was an awesome film, the cinematographer made the ocean by New Zealand look so gorgeous that I knew if I ever had the opportunity to go there, I'd jump.

The drinking age in New Zealand is eighteen, and being that I just celebrated my eighteenth birthday less than a month before, I thought I'd head over to a bar and have a beer with Shyamali, which struck me as a very adult thing to do: have a drink with your sister in a foreign country. Before I could even order, a guy in his twenties came over and yelled, "*Are you Sanjaya from* American Idol*?!*"

So much for anonymity. I said to him, "We're in New Zealand. How do you know that?"

"They're just starting to show the new season here," he said, smiling, "and you're doing great, and we all hope you win, and can we buy you and your sister some drinks?" Okay, being recognized in a foreign country when you're trying to keep a low profile wasn't *all* bad.

Shyamali and I have always been the outdoorsy types— growing up in both the Northwest and Hawaii will do that to you—so we took advantage of what the country had to offer, for instance, white-water rafting in the Nile River and hiking around Mangere Mountain. Aside from having drinks foisted upon us by the locals, the highlight of the trip was my first skydive, a moment of peace so profound that I gained back the ten years of my life that I'd lost from all the stressing I'd done before, during, and after *American Idol*. For a few moments, the last nine months seemed a long, mostly beautiful, but sometimes scary dream. But back on the ground, it was back to reality. I knew that at some point in my life, I'd have to find a way to feel that sort of at-oneness without having to jump out of an airplane.

Ultimately, the whole idea of the trip was to decompress and reflect on the entire experience. I knew that I wouldn't have a real opportunity to do that at home, because when you're at home, you always have something going on. Think about it: how often do you get a chance to zone out and let your mind drift away? Barely ever. There're always errands to do, phone calls to return, and relatives to visit.

Right at that point, I didn't have any ideas on how to move forward with my career, other than to write a few songs with Shyamali. Music is the glue that holds our souls together, and she's my eternal collaborator; even if we're not composing or performing as a unit, we'll always be there in spirit. We managed to write three songs in New Zealand, which, if nothing else, established the sound we were looking for: a world music vibe with a taste of jazz, lounge, and R & B. Shyamali was our lyricist, but I threw in my two cents. The tune we were happiest with is called "Tell Me Who I Am":

Everyone take a look at me
A singer a dreamer an oddity
Take out your notebooks and write this down
'Cause you predicted I'd be out in the first round
It isn't simple as it may have seemed
To fight for what you love and the space in between
But if you step back I can make you see
Just what I really mean
I'm just fine
And I don't need your couch critiquing anymore

Tell me who I am
You seem to know this better than me
An instant expert in my every move
You don't know this life

Your judgment won't wreak havoc on me
'Cause I won't let this mark the end

I made it this far just by being humble
A value of that is more than I knew
Now I push back on those pulling me under
Take your bad press it's a personal view
Take your gloves off and put it on me
I have the conviction to know what you throw
those empty words left to leave me wondering
Will never convince me to stop the show
I'm just fine
And I don't need your couch critiquing anymore

We had some recording equipment with us, so we laid down demo versions of the tunes, with me doing the vocals in the bathroom. (You have to sing in the space with the best acoustics—like the garage over at the *American Idol* hotel—no matter if the area is used for parking cars or taking showers.) In terms of what to do with these songs, there wasn't any kind of grand plan, other than that Shyamali and I would work separately as solo artists for a while, then come together a year or three down the line. I just took things one day at a time. Besides, without any tangible professional opportunities, there was only so much planning I could do. When it came to showbiz, *Idol* gave up plenty of information on how to handle the *show*, but none about how to deal with the *biz*, so I was on my own.

We returned to the States on Halloween day 2007, and there wasn't much to come back to. Nobody in the entertainment industry had any way to contact me—I didn't have an

IMDb page, a website, or a PR flack—so it wasn't like managers, lawyers, or record labels were beating down the door. But that was cool. Having a blank slate, having to start from scratch and build it up with just my family in my corner, wasn't necessarily a bad thing.

I spent a full week hanging out with friends of mine who really didn't care about *Idol*, trying to get into an I'm-just-Sanjaya-from-the-block mode. I wanted to become 100 percent real again. Not that I was too far out in space, but I knew there was some residual rust I had to shake off. For instance, when you're on a major tour, you're catered to a whole lot, so I had to get used to doing everything for myself again. But it wasn't too big of a deal—like I said, I only needed a week. Some people need years. Some people *never* go back to normal.

Taking Simon, Randy, and Paula's suggestion to heart, I tracked down a vocal coach, and for the first time really worked on singing technique. We worked on singing from the diaphragm, she gave me a bunch of warm-up and strengthening exercises, and I learned all the stuff that six-year-olds learn in their first singing lessons.

She was so happy with my progress that one month later, she set up a showcase at a church in Seattle so that prospective managers, lawyers, and investors could hear how far I'd progressed. I reprised "The Way You Make Me Feel" from the tour, and I also sang "You Were Always on My Mind" by Willie Nelson (but Fantasia's version), and "We Are the World." (I didn't want to perform a cappella, because it would've felt too much like an *American Idol* audition, so I had my teacher put together instrumental backing tracks.) I focused on keeping the songs grooving, and on staying in the pocket and utilizing all my new vocal techniques. I'm usually hard on myself, but I thought it went well. The crowd seemed to enjoy it, and that's all that mattered.

One woman in particular really liked it. And that's how I found my first manager.

She had a great vibe about her. She was a lawyer, but she didn't act like one. She was a nurturer with children and a bunch of animals. Having never had a manager before, I didn't know what to expect from her. She signed me up for dance classes, and more vocal coaching, and some comedy workshops. But she wasn't utilizing the *Idol* exposure in the most efficient way, so we let her go.

That's something they never tell you about on *American Idol*—or anywhere else, for that matter: in the entertainment industry, when you're first starting out, even if you were on the top-rated television show in the world, it's unbelievably difficult to find a good representative. Some are dishonest, some are inexperienced, and some don't carry enough weight. And it's impossible to know whether you made the right choice until further down the line. It's like moving into a new house: it looks and feels great at first, but six months later, you find out that the floor squeaks in certain places, and the hot water doesn't always stay hot, and the next-door neighbor's heavy metal band rehearses at his place every Thursday. (The good news is that, after two more lousy managers, I finally found a good one. *Phew!*)

Frustrated with the direction (or lack of direction) our careers were taking (or not taking), Shyamali and I moved to Los Angeles. We rented a beautiful three-bedroom, two-bathroom house with one of the coolest kitchens I've ever had the pleasure to cook in. There was also a pool in the backyard, and a guesthouse that we turned into a makeshift recording studio. We stayed in L.A. for a couple months, but nothing was shaking in the city, so it was back home to Seattle for Shyamali, and back to New York for me.

My highest-profile post-*Idol* gig was one of the most enjoyable: a commercial for Nationwide Insurance shot on location in India. It was a goofy one, no doubt.

- Shot one: Me singing outside of a monastery, daytime, beautiful sun.
- Shot two: Me singing outside of a monastery, nighttime, brutal wind.
- Shot three: Me singing outside of a monastery, nighttime, terrible rainstorm.
- Shot four: Me singing outside of a monastery, morning, beautiful sunrise, hair done up in the ponyhawk.
- Shot five: A monk telling me, "Please, Sanjaya, stop. The guruji will see you now."
- Shot six: Me walking into the monastery, greeted by the sight of rows and rows of praying monks.
- Shot seven: Me standing in front of a holy man with a loooooooong white beard, saying, "Oh, great guruji, please help me. I've tasted fame and fortune. Girls adore me. But I still feel that there's something missing. Tell me: what is the most important thing in life?"
- Shot eight: The guruji staring me down, saying, "A good retirement plan. And a haircut."

Between that and the funnyordie.com video, nobody could accuse me of taking myself too seriously.

And it's a good thing that I don't take things too seriously, because if I did—if I let the entertainment industry dictate what I was and who I should be—I'd probably go a little nuts.

It takes a lot of inner strength to stay grounded while people who have money and power tell you how wonderful you are, and while strangers want you to pose for pictures, and when people get angry at you when it turns out that you're not who they think you should be.

Phil Stacey

What I admired most about Sanjaya was that I don't think there was ever a point where he cared what anybody else thought about him. He was out there to have fun and do his own thing. Every single week I went out there, and I was so nervous, and it was always fun to watch Sanjaya, because he just went out there and had a good time. I wished I could've gotten to that place. He's a positive person to be around. He loves everybody. With everything that happened, he could've developed some bitterness toward a lot of people, and become hardened and jaded. But he didn't care. He just loves people, and he cherished the whole experience. And through all the criticism and the praise, nothing has changed his character.

I'd like to believe that throughout the entire process—from being told I had ADHD; to getting cut, then being brought back during the *Idol* auditions; to shockingly making it to the Top 10; to appearing on TV talk shows I'd been watching my entire life; to touring the country; to being let go by 19 Entertainment; to picking myself up, dusting myself off, and moving forward with my life and career as best I can—I've remained true to myself. And I'd like to think I'll continue to do so, regardless of whether my music, my acting, or my modeling reaches ten people or ten million people.

Here's the lesson that everybody—musicians, viewers, haters, *everybody*—should take from *American Idol:* It's not just about the singing, the clothes, the hair, or the verbal skills to banter with television stars. It's also about honesty, integrity, positivity, delivering the goods, and chillability . . . you know, the whole package.

And by the whole package, I mean *the whole package.* Inside, outside, and everywhere in between.

Log on to www.simonandschuster.com to get an
exclusive preview
of Sanjaya's new song, "Tell Me Who I Am."

To keep up with the world of Sanjaya, be sure to check out
www.sanjayamalakar.com.

Printed in the United States
By Bookmasters